TABLE OF CONTENTS

ECONOMIC RESEARCH CENTRE

90 0400495 7

REPORT OF THE
HUNDRED AND EIGHTH ROUND TABLE
ON TRANSPORT ECONOMICS

held in Paris on 13th-14th November 1997
on the following topic:

WHAT MARKETS ARE THERE FOR TRANSPORT BY INLAND WATERWAYS?

EUROPEAN CONFERENCE OF MINISTERS OF TRANSPORT

EUROPEAN CONFERENCE OF MINISTERS OF TRANSPORT (ECMT)

The European Conference of Ministers of Transport (ECMT) is an inter-governmental organisation established by a Protocol signed in Brussels on 17 October 1953. It is a forum in which Ministers responsible for transport, and more specifically the inland transport sector, can co-operate on policy. Within this forum, Ministers can openly discuss current problems and agree upon joint approaches aimed at improving the utilisation and at ensuring the rational development of European transport systems of international importance.

At present, the ECMT's role primarily consists of:

- helping to create an integrated transport system throughout the enlarged Europe that is economically and technically efficient, meets the highest possible safety and environmental standards and takes full account of the social dimension;
- helping also to build a bridge between the European Union and the rest of the continent at a political level.

The Council of the Conference comprises the Ministers of Transport of 39 full Member countries: Albania, Austria, Azerbaijan, Belarus, Belgium, Bosnia-Herzegovina, Bulgaria, Croatia, the Czech Republic, Denmark, Estonia, Finland, France, the Former Yugoslav Republic of Macedonia (F.Y.R.O.M.), Georgia, Germany, Greece, Hungary, Iceland, Ireland, Italy, Latvia, Lithuania, Luxembourg, Moldova, Netherlands, Norway, Poland, Portugal, Romania, the Russian Federation, the Slovak Republic, Slovenia, Spain, Sweden, Switzerland, Turkey, Ukraine and the United Kingdom. There are five Associate member countries (Australia, Canada, Japan, New Zealand and the United States) and three Observer countries (Armenia, Liechtenstein and Morocco).

A Committee of Deputies, composed of senior civil servants representing Ministers, prepares proposals for consideration by the Council of Ministers. The Committee is assisted by working groups, each of which has a specific mandate.

The issues currently being studied – on which policy decisions by Ministers will be required – include the development and implementation of a pan-European transport policy; the integration of Central and Eastern European Countries into the European transport market; specific issues relating to transport by rail, road and waterway; combined transport; transport and the environment; the social costs of transport; trends in international transport and infrastructure needs; transport for people with mobility handicaps; road safety; traffic management; road traffic information and new communications technologies.

Statistical analyses of trends in traffic and investment are published regularly by the ECMT and provide a clear indication of the situation, on a trimestrial or annual basis, in the transport sector in different European countries.

As part of its research activities, the ECMT holds regular Symposia, Seminars and Round Tables on transport economics issues. Their conclusions are considered by the competent organs of the Conference under the authority of the Committee of Deputies and serve as a basis for formulating proposals for policy decisions to be submitted to Ministers.

The ECMT's Documentation Service has extensive information available concerning the transport sector. This information is accessible on the ECMT Internet site.

For administrative purposes the ECMT's Secretariat is attached to the Organisation for Economic Co-operation and Development (OECD).

Publié en français sous le titre :
QUELS MARCHÉS POUR LES TRANSPORTS PAR VOIES NAVIGABLES ?

Further information about the ECMT is available on Internet at the following address:
http://www.oecd.org/cem/

GERMANY

Karl-Heinz BREITZMANN
Christian WENKE
Institute of Transport and Logistics
University of Rostock
Germany

SUMMARY

Rostock, February 1997

1. PURPOSE AND SCOPE OF THE REPORT

In this report we study the markets for inland waterway transport in Germany. The focus is on the demand side of the freight transport market. The aim is therefore to define the structure and trend of the traffic carried on inland waterways and thus show the position of this transport sector.

The supply side of the market is not examined, as this would have a limiting effect on the analysis of the field concerned. Such issues as the quantitative and qualitative trend of capacity provided and overcapacity problems, the structure of firms and the relationship between shipping companies, owner operators and own-account barge transport, co-operation between forwarders and inland waterway carriers and the impact of deregulation are therefore not included in the study.

In Chapter 2 inland waterway transport is seen in the context of the transport field as a whole. The traffic trend in Germany since the 1950s is analysed. It is also shown that the geographical position of the inland waterways has resulted in an inland waterway system with a marked regional focus.

Inland waterway transport played an outstanding role during the industrial revolution and greatly influenced the pattern of industrial locations. The bulk goods shipped by the mining, iron and steel, heavy machinery, agricultural and other sectors which predominated at that time have declined in importance as the economy branched out into many different directions and as products were increasingly processed. However, in no way does this mean, as is sometimes asserted, that bulk cargoes are no longer of prime importance for inland waterway transport. On the contrary, large quantities of bulk goods are still required, while new kinds of bulk goods have also been produced. This aspect is discussed in Chapter 3 in which the types of goods carried on inland waterways are analysed.

New industrial sectors and products as well as new transport systems and technologies have emerged in the last few years and the global division of labour has given international trade a new basis. The exchange of finished and semi-finished products, supplied parts, modules and spare parts has developed extremely rapidly. The transport sector has been able to meet these challenges only by consolidating loads. In the international field, container transport has revolutionised traditional shipping line services and led maritime transport away from general cargo to modern mass production standards and techniques (Breitzmann, 1993). With the through-transport of containers from the origin and destination points in port hinterlands, inland waterway transport has also found new outlets in which it is competing intensively with road and rail. Chapter 4 examines this aspect and at the same time considers the domestic transport of loading units, particularly in the form of combined traffic.

In the last few years, more and more industrial and trading firms have gone over to extensive logistical systems. A comprehensive approach to procurement, production, distribution and waste disposal processes has resulted in streamlining, lower costs and increased competitiveness. In-house logistical activity is often reduced by outsourcing, which provides new complex fields of activity for logistical service providers. Chapter 5 shows the existing possibilities for inland waterway transport in this context by means of examples.

Chapter 6 discusses the change in the situation which has come about with the unification of Germany and the opening-up of central and eastern Europe. In this connection inland waterway transport in eastern Germany with its links to the South and East and combined river/maritime transport are discussed.

2. LONG-TERM TRENDS AND REGIONAL STRUCTURE OF INLAND WATERWAY TRANSPORT IN GERMANY

Freight transport in Germany has been increasing for several decades. Traffic on long- and short-distance routes in 1992 totalled 3.7 billion tonnes, or 432 per cent of the figure for the base year 1950 (see Table 1)[1]. If short-distance road freight is excluded from total transport, the transport of about one billion tonnes represents an increase to 241 per cent, which corresponds to a rise of tonne-kilometres to 354 per cent or 322 per cent without short-distance road traffic compared with 1950.

Table 1. **Trend in total domestic transport and inland waterway transport in Germany**

		1950[1]	1960	1970	1980	1990	1992[3]
Total transport	mill. t	688.6	1 691.7	2 844.5	3 229.0	3 459.1	3 660.8
	growth[2]		9.4	5.3	1.3	0.7	2.9
	bill. t-km	70.4	142.0	215.3	322.9	300.2	319.6
	growth[2]		7.3	4.2	4.1	-0.7	3.1
Total transport (excl. short-distance road km haulage)	mill. t	313.6	601.7	872.5	974.2	1 049.1	1 070.8
	growth[2]		6.7	3.8	1.1	0.7	1.0
	bill. t-km	63.2	120.2	179.2	210.9	250.8	266.5
	growth[2]		6.6	4.1	1.6	1.7	3.1
Inland waterway transport	mill. t	71.9	172.0	240.0	241.0	231.0	224.1
	growth[2]		9.1	3.4	0.0	-0.4	-1.5
	bill. t-km	16.7	40.4	48.8	51.4	54.8	56.1
	growth[2]		9.2	1.9	0.5	0.6	1.2

1. Excluding Saarland and West Berlin.
2. Average annual growth rate.
3. Old *Länder*.
Source : Unless otherwise stated : *Verkehr in Zahlen, versch. Jahre, herausgegeben vom Bundesministerium*, Bonn.

With 211 million tonnes in 1993, domestic inland waterway traffic was also up considerably from 1950 (to 194 per cent). As in total long-distance transport, traffic expressed in tonne-kilometres rose more rapidly than the transport tonnage (213 per cent).

In 1992 total freight transport accounted for 319.6 billion t-km and total freight excluding short-distance road freight for 266.5 billion t-km.

Over time, however, inland waterway traffic shows considerable differences compared with total domestic traffic. After above-average increases in the 1950s, growth in the 1960s was already under that for total traffic. This low growth was followed by a period of stagnation in inland waterway traffic in the 1970s and a decline in the 1980s, a trend which continued into the early 1990s. Owing to the increasing transport distances, there was also a slight increase in inland waterway t-km in the last few decades. In all, inland waterway transport accounted in 1995 for a domestic total of 237.9 million tonnes or 64 billion t-km, which corresponded roughly to the figure at the start of the 1980s for the old Federal Republic (cf. Lüüs, 1996).

According to surveys by the Ifo Institute for Economic Research, a decrease to 222 million tonnes (59 billion t-km) was recorded in 1996, mainly as a result of unfavourable weather at the start of the year (DVZ No. 149/1996).

Figure 1. **Modal split in domestic traffic**

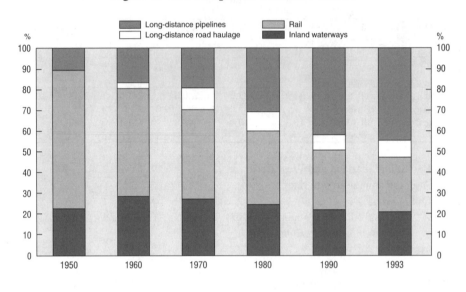

Up to the start of the 1960s, inland waterway transport improved its modal split position (Figure 1). Then its share in traffic fell from 29 per cent in 1960 to 21 per cent in 1993 in terms of tonnage and from 34 per cent to 22 per cent in terms of t-km. However, a further decrease in traffic share has been avoided so far in the 1990s.

Inland waterway transport is associated with a medium transport distance, which in the 1970s was about 200 km and rose to 236 km by 1990, while rail was at 200 km and long-distance road haulage at 275 km. With Germany's unification, the average inland waterway transport distance has risen further in the last few years (1995: 269 km) (BDB 2, 1996).

Even if inland waterway transport is still seen as best suited for long-distance traffic owing to its economic characteristics, more than a tenth of all freight is carried over distances of up to 50 km and over a third on those up to 100 km (see Annex 1). But the share of the lower distance categories is declining in absolute and relative terms. In the period 1980-90, cargo gains in absolute terms were recorded only in the distance bracket exceeding 400 km.

It is becoming clear that rail has recorded marked losses in its position over the entire reference period. If the data for total transport excluding short-distance road haulage is taken as a basis, rail's share decreased from 62 per cent in 1950 and 44 per cent in 1960 to 21 per cent in 1993 (in terms of t-km). Pipeline transport reached a high in the early 1970s and, following a decline during the oil crisis, has kept to a share of 5 per cent in recent years. Road haulage has therefore taken over not only the traffic growth of other transport modes but has also eaten into their shares.

The German markets for inland waterway transport are marked to a considerable extent by international traffic which consists of cross-border and through traffic. This is due both to the geographical structure of the inland waterways and to the focus of inland waterway transport on bulk goods, which are mostly imported by German industry from overseas.

Table 2. **Place of inland waterway transport in Germany's international traffic**

		1950[1]	1960	1970	1980	1990	1993[2]
Total inland waterway traffic	mill. t	104.2	251.8	374.2	394.9	395.5	360.3
(domestic + international)	bill. t-km				86.8	94.8	99.1
International traffic[3]							
Total (excl. sea and air	mill. t	59.0	150.0	320.4	409.3	491.8	477.4
transport)	bill. t-km				92.3	125.3	127.9
Inland waterways	mill. t	32.3	79.8	134.2	153.9	164.5	149.1
	bill. t-km				35.4	40.0	43.0
Share of inland waterways in	basis t	54.7	53.2	41.9	37.6	33.4	31.2
Total international traffic (%)	basis t-km				38.4	31.9	33.6
International inland waterway							
Traffic as % of total inland	basis t	31.0	31.7	35.9	39.0	41.6	41.4
waterway traffic	basis t-km				40.8	42.2	43.4

1. Excluding Saarland and West Berlin.
2. Old *Länder* only.
3. Cross-border and through traffic, excluding traffic to and from West Berlin and the German Democratic Republic.

International traffic has become more important for inland waterway transport over the years. Table 2 shows that the share of international traffic in total inland waterway traffic rose from 31 per cent in 1950 and 31.7 per cent in 1960 to 39 per cent in 1980 and 41.4 per cent in 1993 (on a tonnage basis). Only a slightly higher value was recorded on the basis of t-km.

13

Inland waterways are better placed in the breakdown for international traffic than in that for total transport, for the inland waterways accounted in 1993 for 31.2 per cent of the total international tonnage. But here again, a marked decline is to be seen, since they were still taking over 50 per cent in 1950 and 1960.

Figure 2 clearly shows that international road haulage traffic has also increased extremely rapidly, while rail was up to only 40 per cent (in terms of tonnes) or 58 per cent (in terms of t-km) of inland waterway traffic.

The inland waterway share in German freight traffic has changed since the unification of Germany in 1990 as this transport sector played a considerably less important role in the Democratic Republic than in the Federal Republic.

Figure 2. **Modal split for international traffic**

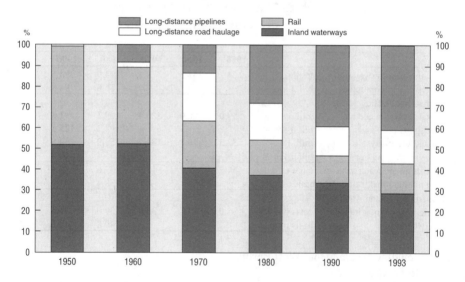

According to Table 3, the inland waterway share in the tonnage carried in East Germany never exceeded 5 per cent. The share in terms of t-km performed was even lower, since relatively short transport distances predominated (on average 113 km in 1989).

14

Table 3. Trend in total transport and inland waterway transport in the Democratic Republic or eastern Germany

		1970	1980	1989	1990*	1991*	1992*	1993*	1994*
Inland waterway	Mill. T	13.7	16.3	20.4	13.6	5.2	6.0	7.4	7.9
	Bill.t-km	2.4	2.2	2.3	1.9	0.9	1.2	1.5	1.7
Rail	Mill. T	262.9	311.6	339.3	234.8	111.8	86.2	83.9	77.8
	Bill.t-km	41.5	56.4	59.0	40.9	17.8	13.6	13.0	...
Long-distance Road haulauge	Mill. T	...	43.6	27.6	18.0	28.7	60.2	60.0	...
	Bill.t-km	...	8.6	7.0	6.2	8.0	16.1	16.6	...
Long-distance Pipelines	Mill. T	15.4	41.6	38.2	29.8	14.2	14.9	15.6	16.8
	Bill.t-km	2.2	5.0	4.3	3.3	2.4	2.4	2.4	2.7
Total	Mill. T	...	413.1	425.5	296.2	160.0	167.3	166.9	...
	Bill.t-km	...	72.2	72.6	52.3	29.1	33.2	33.5	...
Transport sector shares (%)									
Inland waterway	Basis t		3.9	4.8	4.6	3.3	3.6	4.4	
	Basis t-km		3.0	3.2	3.6	3.1	3.6	4.5	
Rail	Basis t		75.4	79.7	79.3	69.9	51.5	50.3	
	Basis t-km		78.1	81.3	78.2	61.2	41.0	38.8	
Long-distance Road haulage	Basis t		10.6	6.5	6.1	17.9	36.0	35.9	
	Basis t-km		11.9	9.6	11.9	27.5	48.5	49.6	
Long-distance Pipelines	Basis t		10.1	9.0	10.1	8.9	8.9	9.3	
	Basis t-km		6.9	5.9	6.3	8.2	7.2	7.2	
Total	Basis t		100.0	100.0	100.0	100.0	100.0	100.0	
	Basis t-km		100.0	100.0	100.0	100.0	100.0	100.0	

* Federal Republic -- new *Länder*.
Source: *Statistisches Jahrbuch der DDR, 1989, Verkehr in Zahlen.*

Eastern Germany's waterway network mainly consists of the Rivers Elbe and Oder and the canals or canalised rivers connecting them. The fact that the course of the waterways did not correspond to the main goods flows and that the Elbe was insufficiently developed as the most important waterway limited the role of inland navigation in the national transport system. The necessary resources for proper maintenance of waterways or for development work on them, such as the connection of Port Rostock with the waterway network, were continually lacking, while waterway capacity was never by any means fully used.

As regards the centrally planned and operated fleet, the development of push-towing was mainly encouraged and pioneering work was carried out especially in the development of canal push-towing. Large numbers of canal push-tugs and barges started being built in 1965, and river push-tugs at a later date. Push-towing already accounted in 1970 for more than half the traffic carried, and the proportion rose to 84 per cent in 1989.

Owing to central control over the cargoes and means of transport, it was possible to develop many intermodal transport operations for the main types of goods carried, i.e. construction materials (1989: 48.3 per cent), coal (18.6 per cent) and waste products (16.7 per cent). Under market economy conditions, a great many of these operations could no longer be maintained, especially as there was a massive transfer to road haulage and total transport declined by more than 40 per cent in one year owing to the adjustment crisis affecting the economy. As a result, the inland waterway tonnage fell within two years to a quarter of the 1989 level, but was back up again by 1994 to 38 per cent of that level. But at the same time the average transport distance also rose in the new *Länder* and, at 215 km in 1994, it was only about 50 km shorter than in the old *Länder*.

The regional structure of German waterway transport is marked by the geographical position of the waterways. The Rhine and its tributaries are away out in front. In 1995, the Rhine accounted for 63.4 per cent of inland waterway traffic and the public inland ports in the Rhine region had the same share in total transhipment operations (see Table 4).

Table 4. **Freight transhipments in public inland ports by waterway region**

Waterway region	1950(a)	1960	1970	1980	1985	1991	1995
	Million tonnes						
Rhine region	61.0	160.8	228.2	215.9	190.4	193.3	183.6
West German canals	23.9	52.4	44.6	39.2	35.3	33.9	36.2
Elbe	5.2	11.9	19.3	17.6	14.1	17.2	23.4
Mittelland Canal region	4.2	11.8	12.0	11.9	12.1	14.6	15.2
Weser	5.5	13.5	17.4	14.7	11.9	11.0	11.9
Berlin (b)	n.a.	4.0	7.3	7.9	7.0	7.8	8.7
Danube	1.4	3.2	4.7	3.4	3.3	2.8	7.2
Brandenbg./Mecklenburg-V.	--	--	--	--	--	2.6	3.6
Mecklenburg-Vorp. Coast	--	--	--	--	--	0.1	0.1
Total	101.2	257.6	333.5	310.6	274.1	283.3	289.9
	% shares						
Rhine region	60.3	62.4	68.4	69.5	69.5	68.2	63.3
West German canals	23.6	20.3	13.4	12.6	12.9	12.0	12.5
Elbe	5.1	4.6	5.8	5.7	5.1	6.1	8.1
Mittelland Canal region	4.2	4.6	3.6	3.8	4.4	5.2	5.2
Weser	5.4	5.2	5.2	4.7	4.3	3.9	4.1
Berlin (b)	-	1.6	2.2	2.5	2.6	2.8	3.0
Danube	1.4	1.2	1.4	1.1	1.2	1.0	2.5
Brandenbg./Mecklenburg-Vorp	--	--	--	--	--	0.9	1.2
Mecklenburg-Vorp. Coast	--	--	--	--	--	0.0	0.0
Total	100.0	100.0	100.0	100.0	100.0	100.0	100.0

(a)   Excluding Saarland and West Berlin;   (b)   West Berlin up to 1990.

West German canals connected with the Rhine rank second, although their share has declined in the long term. The traffic handled in both the Elbe and Mittelland Canal regions has risen considerably, which is no doubt a consequence of the shift in freight flows following unification. The rapid progress of the Danube region following the completion of the Rhine-Main-Danube Canal should also be pointed out. But it is also becoming clear that eastern Germany is taking only a small share of Germany's inland waterway traffic.

3. INLAND WATERWAY MARKETS IN THE CONTEXT OF ECONOMIC STRUCTURAL CHANGE

Taking as a basis the factors defined by Fritz Voigt in 1973 as constituting the economic and operational efficiency of transport, inland navigation is a transport mode which combines high mass transport capacity with low operating costs, an average predictability and good traffic safety, although it is very limited in terms of speed, network development potential and frequency of service.

As seen in the breakdown of freight, bulk goods showing transport affinities corresponding with these characteristics therefore predominate in inland waterway transport. In 1995, the freight categories which together accounted for more than 71 per cent of total traffic were: construction materials (stone and earth: 25 per cent), petroleum products (18 per cent), ores and metal waste (17 per cent) and coal (11 per cent) (see Table 5). In the case of freight categories with much lower shares in traffic, which include chemicals, foodstuffs and animal feed, iron, steel and non-ferrous metals, and agricultural and forestry products as well as fertilisers, inland waterway cargoes also mainly consist of bulk freight, whereas this mode carries a very small share of the more highly processed products belonging to these goods categories, particularly in traffic consisting of vehicles, machinery and semi-finished and finished products (cf. Arnold-Rothmaier, 1966).

Inland waterways play an important role in the transport of dangerous goods, especially those classified as "flammable liquids", as well as "compressed gases, liquefied gases or gases dissolved under pressure". The inland waterway share in total dangerous goods traffic (excluding short-distance road haulage and sea transport) is 34 per cent. Conversely, dangerous goods account for about 23 per cent of inland waterway traffic.

Table 5. **Domestic inland waterway traffic by commodity groups**

Commodity group	1950	1960	1970	1980	1990	1995
	Million tonnes					
Agriculture and forestry products	4.2	8.0	9.1	6.1	7.5	10.2
Foodstuffs and animal feed	2.1	4.8	6.9	9.3	12.9	14.0
Coal	25.9	37.6	24.6	24.0	23.6	26.4
Crude oil	0.9	3.5	1.3	0.7	0.1	0.0
Petroleum products	2.5	17.3	40.3	44.9	40.3	43.3
Ores and metal waste	9.6	30.9	37.5	41.7	41.9	41.0
Iron, steel and non-ferrous metals	3.1	9.2	14.8	14.5	13.3	13.5
Stone and earth	19.1	49.2	87.5	75.0	64.6	59.3
Fertilisers	2.1	5.4	6.2	5.4	7.3	8.1
Chemicals	1.7	4.6	10.1	12.2	16.1	15.2
Vehicles, machinery, semi-finished and finished products	0.7	1.5	1.7	3.6	4.0	6.9
Total	71.9	172.0	240.0	237.4	231.6	237.9
	% shares of commodity groups					
Agriculture and forestry products	5.8	4.7	3.8	2.6	3.2	4.3
Foodstuffs and animal feed	2.9	2.8	2.9	3.9	5.6	5.9
Coal	36.0	21.9	10.3	10.1	10.2	11.1
Crude oil	1.3	2.0	0.5	0.3	0.0	0.0
Petroleum products	3.5	10.1	16.8	18.9	17.4	18.2
Ores and metal waste	13.4	18.0	15.6	17.6	18.1	17.2
Iron, steel and non-ferrous metals	4.3	5.3	6.2	6.1	5.7	5.7
Stone and earth	26.6	28.6	36.5	31.6	27.9	24.9
Fertilisers	2.9	3.1	2.6	2.3	3.2	3.4
Chemicals	2.4	2.7	4.2	5.1	7.0	6.4
Vehicles, machinery, semi-finished and finished products	1.0	0.9	0.7	1.5	1.7	2.9
Total	100.0	100.0	100.0	100.0	100.0	100.0

Table 6. **Trend in domestic freight transport in Germany by commodity group**

Commodity group	1950	1960	1970	1980	1990	1993
	Million tonnes					
Agriculture and forestry products	27.1	41.2	46.2	46.6	52.2	56.6
Foodstuffs and animal feed	12.6	26.6	44.7	76.8	98.5	106.5
Coal	110.5	147.2	120.6	115.9	101.7	113.5
Crude oil	3.0	20.9	84.0	77.9	65.9	84.7
Petroleum products	7.4	33.0	86.5	95.5	93.1	103.5
Ores and metal waste	28.8	78.5	92.7	91.8	82.1	77.0
Iron, steel and non-ferrous metals	20.0	52.7	86.1	94.6	97.7	91.9
Stone and earth	60.3	110.7	151.7	154.8	156.8	171.3
Fertilisers	9.8	19.7	23.3	22.9	17.1	17.1
Chemicals	8.8	21.0	42.7	60.4	80.0	76.4
Vehicles, machinery, semi-finished and finished products	25.3	50.1	93.6	136.1	202.4	225.4
Total	313.6	601.6	872.1	973.3	1 047.5	1 123.9
	Commodity group shares (%)					
Agriculture and forestry	8.6	6.8	5.3	4.8	5.0	5.0
Foodstuffs and animal feed	4.0	4.4	5.1	7.9	9.4	9.5
Coal	35.2	24.5	13.8	11.9	9.7	10.1
Crude oil	1.0	3.5	9.6	8.0	6.3	7.5
Petroleum products	2.4	5.5	9.9	9.8	8.9	9.2
Ores and metal waste	9.2	13.0	10.6	9.4	7.8	6.9
Iron, steel and non-ferrous metals	6.4	8.8	9.9	9.7	9.3	8.2
Stone and earth	19.2	18.4	17.4	15.9	15.0	15.2
Fertilisers	3.1	3.3	2.7	2.4	1.6	1.5
Chemicals	2.8	3.5	4.9	6.2	7.6	6.8
Vehicles, machinery, semi-finished and finished products	8.1	8.3	10.7	14.0	19.3	20.1
Total	100.0	100.0	100.0	100.0	100.0	100.0

The trend in inland waterway transport markets can be explained from the viewpoint of freight categories by the impact of two factors: first, by the "freight structural effect", i.e. by the transfers to the detriment of bulk freight caused by economic structural change; second, by changes in the share of inland waterways in the transport of the various freight categories compared with other transport sectors ("modal economic and operational efficiency effect").

Table 6 illustrates the freight structural effect. If 1993 is compared with 1960, a decrease in absolute terms in the tonnages of coal, ores and metal waste and fertilisers is seen. As the increase in the tonnages of agricultural and forestry products, metals, stone and earth is sub-average, their share in total transport has declined.

Although above-average growth was recorded in the 1950s and 1960s in the freight categories that are decisive for inland waterway transport, their share in traffic has declined considerably since then.

If we consider as a whole the freight categories which have a close affinity with inland waterways, i.e. those in which the waterway share now exceeds 20 per cent, the following average annual percentage growth rates are obtained:

	1950-60	1960-70	1970-80	1980-93
Total traffic	6.0	2.0	0.1	0.0
Inland waterways	9.0	3.4	0.3	-1.1

Traffic involving freight categories that have a close affinity with inland waterways has therefore marked time since the 1970s, even taking into account the fact that transport demand was particularly low in the crisis year of 1993. Since the 1970s, growth rates have been lower than for total traffic.

By contrast, traffic involving processed goods, which have but little affinity with inland waterway transport, have seen the highest growth in total traffic. Tonnages rose from 1970 to 1993 by 141 per cent for vehicles, machinery, semi-finished and finished products, by 138 per cent for foodstuffs and animal feed and by 79 per cent for chemicals.

The highest growth for inland waterways in the last 25 years was also in this range of goods, but it was still less than for total traffic, so that the waterway share in the transport of these goods, which was in any case smaller, declined further. The freight structural effect is therefore an important reason for the decrease in the inland navigation share in domestic freight transport.

The shifts between freight categories are the reflection in the transport field of national and world economic structural changes.

First, the place of the primary sector has continued to decline to the benefit of the secondary sector in market economy countries in the last few decades. Second, enterprises producing more highly processed goods in both the primary and secondary sectors have taken the lead to the detriment of material- and transport-intensive basic industries.   Third, the tertiary sector has seen above-average growth and now accounts for over 40 per cent of GDP in Germany.   Annex 2 makes this trend clear with structural data for the German economy.

Raw material imports by market economy countries grew very rapidly in world trade in the 1950s and 1960s. But, in the last few decades, globalisation of the division of labour has led to faster growth in more highly processed goods. This is shown by Table 7 on Germany's cross-border freight transport.

Table 7. **Cross-border traffic by commodity groups***

Commodity group	1988				1993			
	Import		Export		Import		Export	
	Mill. t	%	Mill. t	%	Mill. t	%	Mill. t	%
Agriculture and forestry products	15.9	6.2	9.2	5.9	19.0	6.2	13.0	7.6
Foodstuffs and animal feed	19.8	7.8	13.5	8.6	21.3	6.9	16.5	9.7
Coal	7.3	2.9	11.1	7.1	14.2	4.6	4.4	2.6
Crude oil	48.9	19.2	0.0	0.0	68.1	22.1	0.0	0.0
Petroleum products	31.8	12.5	5.5	3.5	32.3	10.5	8.6	5.0
Ores and metal waste	41.2	16.2	6.2	3.9	32.4	10.5	8.5	5.0
Iron, steel and non-ferrous metals	16.4	6.4	16.5	10.5	17.7	5.7	17.2	10.1
Stone and earth	23.3	9.2	39.5	25.1	40.7	13.2	37.6	22.0
Fertilisers	4.5	1.8	3.1	2.0	4.8	1.6	2.6	1.5
Chemicals	18.8	7.4	21.8	13.9	20.4	6.6	22.3	13.1
Vehicles, machinery, semi-finished and finished products	26.7	10.5	30.7	19.5	36.9	12.0	39.9	23.4
Total	254.6	100.0	157.1	100.0	307.9	100.0	170.6	100.0

*   Excluding maritime and air transport, 1993 figures for Germany as a whole.

The economic and operational efficiency effect as the second influencing factor is shown by analysing the trend of inland waterway shares in the domestic transport of the various **commodity groups** over time (see Table 8).

It can be seen that the inland waterway share precisely in its leading freight category of stone and earth fell from 57.7 per cent in 1970 to 48.4 per cent in 1980 and to 31.8 per cent in 1993, while the share of petroleum products was also down. The only uptrend in the shares is in ores and metal wastes and fertilisers, while the share in coal transport has remained at around 20 per cent since 1970.

In cross-border freight, inland waterway imports are twice the volume of exports, in keeping with the different structure of goods in the import and export sides and the suitability of inland waterways for bulk freight. A second factor which contributes to this imbalance is the advantageous position of the ports in the mouth of the Rhine in relation to Germany's major bulk freight importing regions. This imbalance was less marked in the past when German seaports had a higher share in bulk freight imports, especially in the case of ores.

The inland waterways also have high shares in the cross-border transport of bulk goods and, in all cases, they are higher than in domestic transport. The waterways have a particularly strong position in the case of petroleum products, ores and metal waste, fertilisers, coal and stone and earth. Their share in the transport of processed goods is also higher than in domestic traffic, but has decreased considerably.

In order to assess the overall impact of the two influencing factors, the inland waterway shares in total traffic and in freight categories for the years 1960 and 1970 can be applied to the year 1990.

If the inland waterways had kept their 1970 share of 27.5 per cent of total traffic, inland waterway traffic in 1990 would have amounted to 288 million tonnes (actual value 231 million tonnes). The difference of 57 million tonnes from the actual tonnage can be attributed, according to a model computation, to:

--	the commodity structural effect with	33 million tonnes and
--	the intermodal competition effect with	24 million tonnes.

Without overrating the results of this estimate, it can be concluded that, if growth in inland waterway traffic has remained less than that for Germany's total traffic, the fact can be explained to roughly the same extent by the declining importance of bulk freight and the increasing competitiveness of road haulage, even for freight which has close affinities with inland waterway transport.

Table 8. Inland waterway shares in domestic and cross-border transport*

Inland waterway share in domestic traffic (%)						
Commodity group	1950	1960	1970	1980	1990	1993
Agricultural and forestry products	15.5	19.4	19.7	13.1	14.4	15.0
Foodstuffs and animal feed	16.7	18.0	15.4	12.1	13.1	11.6
Coal	23.4	25.5	20.4	20.7	23.2	21.2
Crude oil	30.0	16.7	1.5	0.9	0.2	0.1
Petroleum products	33.8	52.4	46.6	47.0	43.3	41.6
Ores and metal waste	33.3	39.4	40.5	45.4	51.0	49.2
Iron, steel and non-ferrous metals	15.5	17.5	17.2	15.3	13.6	14.0
Stone and earth	31.7	44.4	57.7	48.4	41.2	31.8
Fertilisers	21.4	27.4	26.6	23.6	42.7	39.8
Chemicals	19.3	21.9	23.7	20.2	20.1	17.3
Vehicles, machinery, semi-finished and finished goods	2.8	3.0	1.8	2.6	2.0	2.3
Total	22.9	28.6	27.5	24.4	22.1	19.5

Inland waterway share in cross-border traffic (%)						
	1964		1980		1993	
	Imports	Exports	Imports	Exports	Imports	Exports
Agricultural and forestry products	31.9	12.4	21.9	10.1	12.2	21.2
Foodstuffs and animal feed	49.4	41.1	46.8	19.5	32.9	16.8
Coal	45.9	25.5	45.7	36.7	52.9	25.1
Crude oil	2.7	-	0.6	0.0	0.0	0.0
Petroleum products	86.4	61.1	65.3	43.1	64.6	53.5
Ores and metal waste	73.7	26.7	83.3	33.3	88.7	48.0
Iron, steel and non-ferrous metals	40.4	42.7	32.2	38.0	17.5	36.3
Stone and earth	44.4	67.3	51.0	60.8	30.2	44.4
Fertilisers	84.4	70.7	51.0	44.8	60.9	54.0
Chemicals	39.9	39.9	28.7	20.1	22.7	16.6
Vehicles, machinery, semi-finished and finished goods	18.3	10.9	4.2	10.5	3.3	4.3
Total	45.6	39.9	38.9	35.3	29.4	26.5

* Excluding maritime and air transport.

4. COMBINED TRANSPORT AND INLAND WATERWAYS

The basic message in Chapters 2 and 3 is that the inland waterways' traditional markets are shrinking or at least offer no growth potential. It is often to be heard in the debate on the future of inland waterways that this transport mode is the only one, apart from short-sea shipping, which still has free capacity. In view of congested inner cities and tailbacks on motorways, this is certainly an impressive argument, but it is certainly not strong enough to justify expectations of a breakthrough for inland waterways as a result of a collapse in road haulage traffic. Nor are the advantages of inland waterways in terms of environmental impact leading under the present circumstances to market growth. Action is therefore required from the sector itself as well as from policy decisionmakers. This means that ways must be found of developing new, competitive services and improving the basic conditions of inland waterway transport.

Owing to the structural effects which have been discussed, an extremely important objective is to obtain outlets for inland waterways by focusing on new types of shipments in expanding markets, i.e. those involving more highly processed goods.

The attempt by inland waterways to penetrate the finished and semi-finished goods market is handicapped by two structural disadvantages: their limited speed and their limited network development potential, i.e. the need for breaks in carriage with time-consuming and costly transhipment processes. Inland waterway transport can therefore be successful only in combined transport using loading units, owing to the savings in terms of time and transhipment costs. By including the advantages of road haulage for the collection and distribution of loading units, competitive services can be provided especially when shorter road haulage times can be trumped by lower overall costs. For this purpose it is also necessary to integrate the inland waterways in through-transport chains by means of closer co-operation with forwarders or through-transport services offered by inland waterway operators themselves.

The disadvantage of lower transport speeds on inland waterways is less important in the phases preceding and following sea transport, as proved by the development of container shipping in the hinterland of the Rhine mouth ports.

If the total transport time of a container is 25 to 30 days, two more days of transport are not of great importance if competitiveness is maintained in other respects, particularly in terms of reliability.

Container traffic has therefore also expanded over twenty years, especially on the Rhine from Rotterdam and Antwerp to Basle, with annual growth rates of over 10 per cent. Cross-border container traffic exceeds domestic traffic by a factor of roughly 12 to 1 (see Table 9). Over three-quarters of domestic traffic consists of shuttle traffic between Bremen and Bremerhaven (Lüüs, 1996).

Table 9. **Inland waterway container traffic**

		1994	1995	1994-95 % change
Domestic traffic				
Total	TEU	56 015	51 838	-7.5
Laden	TEU	43 002	41 842	-2.7
	'000 t	396	457	15.4
Empty	TEU	13 013	9 996	-23.2
Cross-border traffic				
Total imports	TEU	274 516	302 589	10.2
Laden	TEU	131 875	159 436	20.9
	1 000 t	1 190	1 527	28.3
Empty	TEU	142 641	143 153	0.4
Total exports	TEU	309 238	297 239	-3.9
Laden	TEU	234 192	247 422	5.6
	1 000 t	2 389	2 652	11.0
Empty	TEU	75 076	49 817	-33.6
Through traffic	TEU	68 647	97 039	41.4
Laden	TEU	...	56 195	...
	1 000 t	...	608 607	...
Empty	TEU	...	40 844	...

1995: Partly estimated.
Source: Lüüs, 1996.

On the Main and the Main-Danube Canal, containers are shipped in two layers to ports on the Danube. There are also container services on the Neckar to Stuttgart (since 1996) and on the Elbe from Hamburg to Prague (operated in the 1980s by Czech vessels and since 1995 as combined German/Czech services). Containers are carried via the coastal canal and the West Frisian waterways between Bremen/Bremerhaven and Rotterdam/Antwerp.

If no major traffic flows have developed so far outside the Rhine routes, this is mainly due to two factors: first, owing to the inland waterways' wide-meshed network, transport distances compared with road or rail are rapidly increasing. Second, bridges and lock dimensions limit the number of possible containers per vessel. For instance, in traffic to the Rhine region from Hamburg and Bremen, 88 TEU at most can be loaded and only one layer of containers can be carried at present on runs to Berlin, while as many as 210 TEU in four layers per vessel can be shipped on the Rhine (Zimmermann, 1996). The competitiveness of inland waterway container traffic could be further improved if vessels were introduced that could take four containers side by side and thus fully use the widespread lock width of 12 metres.

Owing to the limitations on shipping because of the water level fluctuations on the Elbe, alternative transport possibilities had to be planned before the start of regular services so that reliable operation could be guaranteed. Two layers can be carried at average low water flow and three layers in some sections at low water. Draft limitations are of little importance in container shipping since full deadweight capacity is seldom used, owing to the high proportion of empty containers (31.3 per cent in 1995).

Cost comparisons between modes on important routes from Hamburg have shown that on one-way hauls the barge has marked advantages in terms of costs compared with the lorry, while the advantages compared with rail are considerably reduced, or rail is cheaper for transport to Dortmund. If it is borne in mind, however, that the lorry has many possibilities for return freight, the advantage to inland waterways is considerably smaller for return journeys (Zimmermann, 1996).

The rapid development of combined traffic on inland waterways can be seen from the transhipment data for inland ports given in Table 10. The share in cargo volume of about 3 per cent is still low but, owing to the higher freight rates, its impact is considerably greater for the operators.

Table 10. Combined traffic handled at public inland ports

		1991	1992	1993	1994	1995	Average annual growth 1991-95 (%)
Waterside transhipment							
Containers	TEU	452 000	401 000	469 948	519 234	690 712	11.2
	1000t	2 557.0	2 383.0	2 977.9	3 683.2	4 219.3	13.3
Ro/Ro traffic							
Vehicles without loads	No.	90 715	164 614	140 889	272 508	408 172	45.6
	1000t	178.2	258.5	228.3	352.6	516.3	30.5
Vehicles with loads	No.	4 761	7 117	6 614	7 612	3 974	- 4.4
	1000t	113.2	185.1	175.2	190.7	109.7	- 0.8
Heavy and bulk consignments	No.	228	959	1 075	179	231	0.3
	1000t	9.8	34.6	56.0	8.8	16.4	13.8
Ro/Ro total	No.	95 704	172 690	148 578	280 299	412 377	44.1
	1000t	301.2	478.2	459.5	552.1	642.4	20.8
Total	No.	547 704	573 690	618 526	799 533	1 103 089	19.1
	1000t	2 858.2	2 861.2	3 437.4	4 235.3	4 861.7	14.2
Railside transhipment							
Containers	TEU	229 000	201 940	195 027	207 987	265 337	3.8
	1000t	1725.0	1926.4	1650.9	1838.6	2306.2	7.5
Swap bodies	No.	22 000	81 000	144 729	162 293	161 064	64.5
	1000t	391.0	1331.0	1680.4	1935.9	1898.8	48.4
Trailers	No.	8 000	22 132	28 060	35 825	28 582	37.5
	1000t	120.0	385.1	499.6	638.3	494.8	42.5
Total	No.	259 301	305 550	368 276	406 657	455 625	15.1
	1000t	2 236.0	3 642.5	3 830.8	4 412.9	4 699.8	20.4
Total combined traffic	No.	807 005	879 240	986 802	1 206.190	1 558 714	17.9
	1000t	5 094	6 504	7 268	8 648	9 562	17.0

Source: Bundesverband Öffentlicher Binnenhäfen, authors' calculations.

The growth rates are still higher for Ro/Ro traffic although it represents only 15 per cent of container traffic loads since the transport of empty vehicles predominates, while conventional Ro/Ro involving the transport of loaded trailers plays a minor role. Vehicles are thus carried from the Ford works in Cologne by barge to the distribution centre in Neuss. Since 1995 a firm specialising in logistical operations for the car industry has been operating a Ro/Ro service on the Danube with three push-tugs and eight barges between Regensburg and Budapest, with ports of call at Vienna and Bratislava. In addition to vehicles produced in Germany, imported vehicles are also shipped via Bremerhaven. On the return journey vehicles are loaded in Budapest and Bratislava. In 1996 about 40 000 units were carried (DVZ No. 141/1996).

New demands are being placed on inland ports as a result of combined transport. Owing to the present structure of the sector, the inland ports have to be equipped with container transhipment facilities and developed into junction points in the container transport chain if efficient regular container services are to be built up on the inland waterways (ECMT, 1990, p. 40). The ports and their regional authorities must take responsibility for the necessary development of infrastructure, since the inland waterway operators, with the exception of a few major companies, do not have the necessary capital for this purpose.

Most public ports have sidings and transhipment facilities for combined traffic. They are thus to be seen as junction points in combined transport, as is proved by the transhipment figures for rail/road transport. Many ports on the Rhine, the Main and the Main-Danube Canal already have special container transhipment equipment. In 1994, out of a total of over 100 public inland ports, more than 30 were equipped for container traffic, 17 with Ro/Ro facilities and 14 with facilities for combined rail/road traffic (Walther, 1995). It is therefore possible to develop inland ports into goods traffic centres and to guarantee a connection with inland waterways when new centres are set up.

A goods traffic centre is a transhipment site operated by service providers with logistical functions. Goods are collected and distributed by the centre. This is also the simplest conventional description of a port, if it is also said that a port handles ships. What is new in this system is that the focus is no longer on the carrier but on the load, for which services are provided, irrespective of the carrier. Ports are still interfaces between different carriers and therefore logistical junction points. The location of many inland ports near town centres can therefore be a considerable advantage.

Inland waterway and port operators have realised the possibilities that are open and have worked out valid system concepts. The continual complaint is that they are given too little attention in transport policy, especially by Deutsche Bahn AG, and that goods traffic centres are set up without waterway connections, even at sites near important waterways, as in the case of Magdeburg (BÖB, 1996).

Combined transport plays a central role in the development plans for Duisburg-Ruhrort, Europe's largest inland port. The port handled over 91 000 TEU in 1995. In connection with the Duisburg CombiPort project, a new 210 000 m^2 terminal for combined traffic was built in 1996. Areas are being prepared for further development. In 1995, a development company for the "Duisburg/Lower Rhine decentralised goods traffic centre" was founded, with the port as the cornerstone. Three major logistical enterprises which operate sites near the distributors have already moved into a logistical centre. Import logistics is seen as an expanding activity for the port, which has launched "the Duisburg European Logistics Centre" initiative (ZfB 3/96).

5. INLAND WATERWAYS IN LOGISTICAL SYSTEMS

More and more industrial and trading enterprises are introducing logistical systems in order to cut costs, mainly by optimising their buying, production, distribution and waste disposal operations as well as by outsourcing and, in order to increase their competitiveness, by improving delivery services. Transport, transhipment and warehousing are being treated to an even greater extent as an entity and are being integrated in the basic functions of enterprises, where this can be done with the use of integrated information and communication systems (telematics).

Transport enterprises are therefore confronted with many kinds of challenges. Their markets are becoming more complex in that traditional transport activities are being supplemented by other logistical services. As carriers become operators of complex logistical services, differences are seen between those providing system, composite, special and individual services (Gudehus, 1995).

The centre of the stage in the "logistical revolution" is occupied by industrial and trade sectors which make little use of inland waterway transport. It is all the more important to observe and assess these trends from the viewpoint of the inland waterways in order to identify new opportunities and not be excluded from the new developments.

Since the place of inland waterways and inland ports in logistical systems is undoubtedly a topic in itself, only a few aspects of the subject are addressed here.

Logistics is often associated with the just-in-time principle. As the concept for the time being has mainly caught on in the car industry as a sector where output is geared to assembly, logistics today is still frequently identified with supplies that are ready for the assembly line with little or no prior stocking. It has recently emerged from the debate that what is decisive is not rapid transport, but reliable and predictable transport services which dispense with extensive and costly warehousing. Seen from this angle, inland waterway transport has a definite role to play in logistical systems, and not only with regard to bulk goods.

Since most potential customers for logistical services have no direct access to waterways, it is particularly important that inland ports should become logistical centres. This means that the services provided for goods must go further than the traditional transhipment and storage activities and must include processing. In the phase following sea transport, inland ports, particularly in the Rhine region, therefore have possibilities of taking over services that are traditionally provided at seaports.

Many inland ports, however, are confronted with two problems for the establishment of new service providers or processors for the development of logistical centres:

1. The present user structures, which often have nothing to do with inland waterway transport, can be changed only with difficulty or at considerable cost;
2. Precisely because they are centrally located in towns, many inland ports are limited in terms of further development, as no reserve areas are available, the size of the site is often insufficient for modern transhipment facilities, particularly for container traffic (e.g. Berlin's *Osthafen*), and the cost of development areas is exorbitant (cf. Stackelberg, 1995).

Special functions can be assumed by inland ports and waterways near city centres in connection with urban logistical systems. Many European cities have developed in the vicinity and with the backing of inland waterways, and even today city centres can be easily reached by waterway. The role open to inland waterway transport can be illustrated with the particular problems of construction site logistics in the case of Berlin.

With the major construction projects in the city centre -- the reconstruction of the Potsdamer Platz, government buildings in the curve of the Spree and the Zoo Tunnel -- construction site logistical problems have arisen on a scale seldom seen in city centres. Inland waterway transport can be integrated in the logistical system since the urban region is opened up right into the city centre by the canalised Rivers Havel and Spree and by several canals with unloading depths of between 1.8 and 2 m, and as the building sites lie near or on the waterways.

For the construction site on the Potsdamer Platz alone, which at present is the largest in Europe, it is estimated that within eight years there will be handled 6 million tonnes of excavated material and 1.4 million tonnes of miscellaneous supplies. In response to the transport problems concerned, Baustellenlogistik Potsdamer Platz GmbH has been set up to carry out the following building site activities:

- Collection of all the excavated material and removal by rail or barge for reutilisation or dumping;
- Delivery of ready-mixed concrete;
- Organisation of all the miscellaneous supplies, transhipment operations and transport to the building sites on a just-in-time basis;
- Collection of separated types of building waste, transhipment operations and removal;
- Disposal of excavation water.

All the necessary installations were created at two poorly utilised railway freight stations in the neighbourhood (Maier, 1994).

The Landwehr Canal which runs past the building site is used for inbound and outbound barge transport, although its banks are very narrow and it is flanked by roads which cannot be closed or restricted for traffic. Push-barges are loaded under a conveyor bridge with a 5 m clearance height, and taken to a nearby coupling berth for convoy forming. Dumping into the barge is to a large extent a dust-free and noise-attenuated operation. Up to 4 000 tonnes a day per vessel can therefore be removed (Kirchhoff, 1994). An annual traffic volume of 1 million tonnes is expected for the inland waterways. The daily operation of 15 push-barges of the same size as those normally used on East German waterways reduces traffic in the congested city centre by about 225 lorry journeys.

A crane which can still take 25 tonnes at a 40 m radius has been erected on one of the building sites for the transhipment of miscellaneous freight. The use of barges is especially suitable for the transport of bulky parts such as steel structures, escalators, lifts, etc. (Eichler, 1994).

In the light of these results and traffic congestion in the city, 25 other major construction projects in Berlin have been examined with a view to the use of barges and temporary transhipment berths. For this purpose 22 suitable access points have been identified, as well as eleven locations for unloading building site waste, four of which do not require a final road journey. The basic idea is to use barges for the main transport operation. Equipment variants, which include a special mobile transhipment technique and permit in each case maximum transhipment rates of 400 t/h, have been developed for the temporary transhipment berths. The initial operational results are already available. The greatest transport requirement is for the government and railway buildings in the curve of the Spree (accounting for 6.5 million tonnes of excavated material and 1.25 million m^3 of ready-mixed concrete). Unlike the Potsdamer Platz building site, there is not sufficient capacity in the nearby railway stations, so that rail can take only about 20 per cent of total traffic (Tessmann, 1995).

The role of inland waterways does not, however, have to be limited to the transport of construction materials, excavated earth and construction site waste. In connection with the major Berlin construction sites, the idea has also been proposed for a mobile barge mixing plant which produces 80 m^3/h of concrete and is also supplied by push-barge (Tessmann, 1995).

An especially interesting aspect which emerges from these examples is the definition of complex solutions for a limited period, even including the provision of temporary transhipment sites.

The idea of the floating logistical centre could be studied more closely, precisely in connection with large construction sites [cf. Kieserling (1996) for further examples of the integration of inland waterway transport in logistical systems]. Push-towing, with its relatively cheap transport vessels, is especially appropriate in such systems in which the barge at the same time serves as a storage plant.

Another application worth considering is the removal of refuse by barge in connection with the logistical problems of today's major cities. Refuse was an important commodity for East German inland waterways, especially in the Berlin area. But more work has to be done, particularly on resolving transhipment problems, if sustainable logistical systems are to be developed. In this context, the co-operation of all the parties concerned is a must.

The transport of heavy and oversized cargoes is another specific logistical area for which inland waterways are very suitable. While, in road haulage, loads which are wider than 2.5 m, longer than 20 m and higher than 4 m or heavier than 40 tonnes are already exceptional consignments, such loads are no problem for a modern inland vessel with cargo hold dimensions of 75 x 10 m. By coupling several push barges it is possible to form much larger units, up to the limits set by the particular waterway. Sound experience has also been acquired with the use of flat-deck barges, which are particularly suitable for the Ro-Ro transhipment of heavy goods.

The share of inland waterways in this market does not correspond to their possibilities. There are many reasons why this is so, but if a determined approach is taken to this market segment, the inland waterway share can certainly be increased, which at the same time would relieve pressure on the road network.

6. INLAND WATERWAY TRANSPORT IN EAST GERMANY AND TO EASTERN EUROPE

German reunification and the political upheaval in eastern Europe made it possible to amalgamate the West and East German transport networks that had been formerly separated. The cargo potential in the Elbe-Oder region in the year 2010 was estimated at 45 million tonnes a year at the start of the 1990s, which would mean a twofold increase compared with 1989. The forecast for traffic on the Elbe alone was for 51 million tonnes in the year 2000, or five times the value for 1989.

But problems immediately arose because of the considerably smaller dimensions of the East German waterways. The use of waterways in East Germany is limited by the fact that the Elbe and the Oder, which include extensive stretches of free-flowing water, are subject to marked water-level fluctuations and the existing canals are too narrow for the West German inland waterway fleet. It is forecast that it will take at least twenty years to eliminate these infrastructure shortcomings. According to the 1992 Federal Transport Plan, investments of about DM 30 billion have been set aside for the development of the East German waterways up to the year 2012 (see Figure 3).

The improvement of waterway links with Berlin by completing the Mittelland Canal and developing the Elbe-Havel Canal and the Lower Havel waterway was included as Project 17 in the list of "German Unity Transport Projects". It comprises the construction of a canal bridge over the Elbe at Magdeburg, a double lock as a descent structure to the Elbe-Havel Canal, a lock near the Rothensee ship hoist and the reconstruction of locks on the Elbe-Havel Canal and Berlin. In the follow-up phase, the Havel-Oder waterway (with the new Niederfinow descent structure) and the Hohensaaten-Friedrichsthaler waterway to the lower Oder are to be developed (as an urgent requirement in the 1992 Federal Transport Plan).

Further urgent waterway projects in eastern Germany concern the development of the Elbe and Saale.

The Elbe is the port of Hamburg's traditional link with the hinterland and imports from overseas thus account for a high proportion of the cargo tonnage. As it is the Czech Republic's only waterway link with a seaport, the potential for the development of container traffic prior to and following sea transport is high, in addition to the important role played by conventional inland waterway cargoes. In 1995, 2 050 TEU were carried in the second full year of operation of a joint German/Czech regular service. The potential is estimated at 10 000 TEU by the year 2000 (Horyna, 1996). Building materials extracted in the river valley play an important role in inland waterway freight on the River Elbe. Traffic has increased sharply in the last few years on the river and on its lateral canal. Traffic is mainly impeded by the marked fluctuations in the water level, as only the upper reaches of the Elbe in the Czech Republic are regulated by damming.

Figure 3. **1992 Federal Transport Plan**
-- Federal waterways --

Source: Federal Transport Plan, 1992.

Inland waterway transport in East Germany is concentrated on the Berlin region and on Magdeburg at the interface of the Elbe and Mittelland Canal. Berlin is connected with the Elbe via the Elbe-Havel Canal and the Lower Havel waterway and with the West German canal network and the Rhine via the Mittelland Canal. The Havel-Oder waterway and the Oder-Spree Canal provide the eastward link to the Oder and to the Baltic. The northwards link via the Havel and the Müritz-Havel waterway is of no significance to freight traffic today.

A decentralised port structure has developed on the waterways in the Berlin region, with at present about 100 ports and transhipment points, including 15 public facilities. Prior to reunification, a third of freight in West Berlin and about a fifth in the East was carried by waterway, which resulted in a transhipment at the waterside of 11 to 12 million tonnes (in 1995, about 15 million tonnes in Greater Berlin). A traffic of 21 million tonnes is forecast for the year 2010. Freight mainly consists of traditional bulk goods, in particular construction materials, coal, petroleum products, refuse, iron and steel (Kalender, 1993). The forecasts produced in the early 1990s for the development of inland waterway transport in Eastern Germany are being adjusted as a result of the economic trend which has emerged in the meantime. The decline in traditional industries and only few investments by new customers for inland waterway services, precisely in the Berlin region as well, is reviving the debate on whether there is any point in developing the waterways to Berlin to the level provided for under Project 17. The question posed is therefore **whether the waterways are to be adjusted to the vessels or the vessels to the waterways.**

The conflicting positions should not be seen as alternatives, although waterway development is the only possibility of participating in the inland waterway transport market as far as the existing Rhine-based fleet is concerned. On the other hand, considering the present plans, the time frame for waterway development itself requires ships and utilisation techniques that correspond as closely as possible to the present state of the waterways. This applies to such issues as:

-- low-draft vessels;
-- optimised vessel dimensions and shapes;
-- minimum but functional equipment of the fleet;
-- one-man operation allowing ship design;
-- continuous day and night operation;

--   cargo space designed for the most rapid transhipment time possible (Schönknecht, 1992).

The impact on the natural environment of waterway development frequently assumes proportions resulting in serious conflicts of interest between environmentalists and inland waterway operators. Disputes over the development of the Danube between Straubing and Vilshofen and over work on the lower Elbe suggest that it will probably be very difficult to canalise the middle reaches of the Elbe. The development of the Elbe-Havel Canal and the lower Havel waterway is also encountering considerable opposition from environmental protection associations.

A further obstacle to the speedy development of waterways will probably be the tightness of budgets in the foreseeable future.

Just as in the case of the westwards development of waterways, the link with the Oder via the Havel-Oder and Spree-Oder waterways is extremely important for inland waterway transport in the Berlin region. Despite the existing limitations, these waterways are increasingly used for imports from Poland, particularly for construction materials. The Oder provides a link with Szczecin, the Polish seaport in the Baltic, which in the past played an important role in the economic activity of Berlin as the city's nearest seaport.

According to various studies, a traffic of 4.2 million tonnes is forecast for the Havel-Oder waterway in the year 2010 (1993: 855 kt) as compared with 6-7 million tonnes (1993: 2.1 million tonnes) for the Spree-Oder waterway in the same year, provided these waterways are improved (IVB, 1995).

In addition to waterway improvement, the ports and transhipment sites -- which number over thirty, including twenty on the German side -- in the Oder river system must be further developed, so that they can serve as multimodal interfaces and logistical centres. The following ports in particular can be developed: Eisenhüttenstadt (steel industry), Schwedt (oil refinery, paper industry), Velten, Rüdersdorf, Fürstenwalde, Eberswalde and, on the Polish side, Szczecin (seaport), Kostrzyn, Urad and Krosno.

The economic growth of the Oder region on both sides of the river is of considerable importance for the increase in cargo volume. Industrial activity which was quite intensive on the German side until 1989 has declined sharply and agricultural activity has also decreased considerably. The Polish region around the middle and lower reaches of the Oder is mainly agricultural, with

Gorzów and Szczecin as the only industrial centres. The growth momentum may come particularly from the outer Berlin region, while the frontier acts both as a stimulus and a deterrent (Linde/Tessmann, 1995).

The opening-up of eastern Europe has enlivened the debate on the eastbound operation of inland waterway transport. In particular, access to the efficient Russian waterway network would add a new dimension to European inland navigation.

For this purpose considerable investment in the improvement and reconstruction of waterways would be necessary, particularly in Poland. Polish waterways, with a total length of 4 000 km, mainly comprise the Weichsel and Oder river systems, which are canalised only on their upper reaches. A link between both rivers exists via the Warta, the Notec and the Bydgoski Canal, and the Pripjat and the Dnepr in the Ukraine can be reached via the Bug. As the waterways have not been improved, industrial goods traffic can to all intents and purposes be carried only on the Oder. According to the Polish authorities, the resources for waterway engineering should also be mainly allocated to this river. The creation of an efficient West-East link is not expected in the medium term.

The Danube has good prospects as an efficient waterway for traffic to Slovakia, Hungary and the Balkan countries. Following completion of the Main-Danube Canal, it is possible to reach the Black Sea with modern vessels directly from the Rhine, although the significance of this waterway lies not so much in traffic between the terminal points as in the possibility of directly reaching any one port from any other port over a stretch of 3 500 km. The present situation is, however, mainly marked by policy problems and the decline of the economies in the lower reaches of the river (Arnold-Rothmaier, 1996). The Danube can also be used for combined transport to Greece and the Near East. Sound experience has already been acquired with trailer traffic from Regensburg to the Bulgarian port of Vidin.

River/sea transport, whether with seagoing inland waterway craft or seagoing vessels suitable for inland navigation, is a useful alternative, especially for traffic involving Russia and the Ukraine. The current fleet of vessels available for such transport operations is estimated at 1 400 units, about half of which sail under the Russian flag. The carrying capacity of these vessels is between 1 000 and 4 000 tonnes, and up to 5 000 tonnes in the case of Russian vessels (Wegener, 1996). Since the vessels always have to strike a compromise between the different requirements for use at sea and on waterways, their equipment must correspond to both types of transport and the crews must have the necessary qualifications and licences, they cost much more to build and operate than pure seagoing or inland waterway craft. This higher outlay must be offset by the advantage of avoiding at least one transhipment in a seaport with its associated costs and risks for the cargo. As the level of these savings also depends on the distance which can be covered on a cost-effective basis on inland waterways, inland/coastal shipping is a worthwhile alternative for fragile goods with high transhipment costs, but less so for the bulk freight characteristic of inland navigation.

In western Europe, the main waterway legs for such traffic are the Rhine (particularly up to Duisburg: 1995 -- 2.5 million tonnes handled in public inland ports), the Seine up to Paris (730 000 tonnes) and the Rhone up to Lyons (500 000 tonnes) (Stomberg, 1995). The traffic involving Lakes Vänern and Malaren in Sweden as well as that via the Saimaa Canal in Finland is also substantial. Practically all the countries through which the Danube flows can be reached by seagoing vessels.

The greatest possibilities for river/sea transport are provided by the Russian waterways which, simply because of their dimensions, can be used by larger vessels and permit links with the Baltic, the White Sea, the Black Sea, the Azov Sea and the Caspian Sea. Russia has been operating river/sea services for many years. About 24 million tonnes of cargo a year are carried on these services, including 3 million tonnes to Germany, 11 million tonnes to western Europe and 4 million tonnes to the Mediterranean (ZfB, 1/1996). A direct, regular service from Hamburg to Moscow is thus provided, with a transport time of twelve days. As ships operating under foreign flags do not have access at present to Russian waterways, European inland waterway operators can work only in co-operation with Russian shipping companies.

But river/sea transport can also certainly open up smaller waterways to special kinds of traffic. For example, paper for printing newspapers, which can be damaged very easily during transhipment operations, has been shipped directly to the UK from a paper factory in Schwedt on the Oder. A low-draft river/seagoing vessel, which was fitted out in the port of Szczecin, was used owing to the draft limitations. The trial operation was technically a success, but the limited volume of cargo (700 tonnes as compared with a carrying capacity of 1 700 tonnes) and the small number of vessels with the necessary characteristics rule out permanent services (Linde, 1996).

In addition to the operation of specially built river/seagoing vessels, experience has also been acquired with the use of inland waterway vessels for traffic to and from the coastal areas of the southern Baltic. Following the attempts made by the German Democratic Republic in the late 1960s and early 1970s to operate inland waterway craft in coastal waters on runs as far as Denmark, the use of push-convoys with a specially designed coupling system was tested in the 1980s. It transpired that the use of push-barges on the coast was quite feasible if the tug unit was structurally designed and equipped for this operation. Hatch covers for container ships were recently carried on convoys consisting of two flat-deck barges from a shipyard in Oderberg to the HDW yard in Kiel, via the Havel-Oder waterway, the lower Oder and the Baltic. Polish ports along the Baltic coast could also be served by these vessels, which are available for use as they still have the classification issued by the GDR register of shipping. Legal questions must also be resolved for the sustainable development of traffic carried on inland vessels in Baltic coastal waters, especially if international transport services are to be operated [Linde (*Wettbewerbsperspektiven*), 1996].

On the whole, the development prospects are probably brighter in the longer term for transport to and from eastern Europe with the use of river/seagoing vessels than for transport exclusively by inland waterway.

7. SYNOPSIS

Inland navigation is still an important transport sector, whose share in traffic in Germany has declined in the long term but still stands at about 21 per cent of total freight. Most inland waterway traffic consists of long-distance freight on routes with an average length of 270 km, although the short-distance tonnage is also substantial.

Cross-border and through services account for about 40 per cent of inland waterway traffic. The main cargoes consist of bulk freight which is imported via the ports in the mouth of the Rhine. The Rhine waterways account for almost two-thirds of total traffic.

Inland waterways specialise in bulk freight. Over 70 per cent of their tonnages consists of stone and earth, petroleum products, ores and scrap and coal. Inland navigation also plays an important role in the transport of dangerous goods, since it is used for high tonnages of petroleum products and liquefied gas. It takes smaller shares in freight categories consisting of chemicals, foodstuffs and animal feed, iron, steel and non-ferrous metals, agricultural and forestry products and fertilisers.

The share of inland waterways in Germany's total traffic has declined far less than that of rail. In both cases, the losses are due to structural changes in the national and world economies, as seen in the decreasing proportion of bulk goods suitable for inland waterway transport compared with the rapid growth in more highly processed goods. This "freight structural effect" accounts for some 60 per cent of the loss in the inland waterway share since the 1950s and 1960s. Additionally, the inland waterways have lost traffic shares in some commodity groups, especially to road haulage. This "intermodal competition effect" accounts for about 40 per cent of the decline in their market share.

Inland transport operators should aim not only at defending their traditional freight markets but also at developing their share in growth markets. This applies particularly to processed products in the multimodal transport field. Particularly on the Rhine, inland navigation has developed the container transport market and stimulated traffic with high growth rates. Technical limitations (clearances, lock dimensions) have impeded the rapid development of container traffic on other routes. Combined road/inland waterway traffic can also be expanded by developing more goods transport centres and combined transport terminals in inland ports or in their vicinity.

The integration of inland navigation in logistical systems provides growth opportunities for both bulk freight and miscellaneous goods, wherever reliability is more important than speed. Inland vessels can also be used as storage facilities for logistical centres and serve as a basis for logistical services. The use of inland navigation in city logistical systems makes it possible to reduce road traffic in major areas which have been opened up by waterways. The advantages of inland waterways are particularly marked in the transport of supplies to major building sites and the removal of waste from them.

There is a market potential for inland navigation on routes to and from East Germany and eastern Europe. Full use of this potential means that the waterway network has to be developed, particularly by carrying out the operations coming under Project 17 of the "German Unity Transport Plans". At the same time, the possibilities of optimised vessel design and utilisation concepts should be examined.

In traffic to and from eastern Europe and particularly Russia, western Europe's and Russia's efficient waterway systems can be connected by means of river/seagoing vessel transport. Applications for ad hoc solutions in river/seagoing transport can always be found whenever heavy and outsize loads or cargoes requiring careful handling during transhipment have to be carried.

NOTE

1. Continuous time series for German freight traffic are available only up to 1992 (total transport) or 1993 (excluding short-distance road traffic). In order to ensure the consistency of the time series, data for the old *Länder* are given wherever separate statistics are available. Otherwise, the change in series is shown by a vertical line between the two columns concerned.

ANNEXES

Annex 1. Freight transport by mode and distance bracket

Basis: Goods carried in million tonnes

Distance bracket (km)	Inland waterways 1980	Inland waterways 1990	Rail 1980	Rail 1990	Long-distance road haulage 1980	Long-distance road haulage 1990
0-50	32.2	27.0	135.0	106.1	11.2	16.8
51-100	64.0	59.5	40.8	37.5	36.5	54.6
101-150	30.9	28.2	28.2	24.6	53.9	78.0
151-200	23.7	20.2	21.8	19.4	44.3	60.7
201-250	13.7	12.2	21.9	19.1	30.2	42.6
251-300	10.3	8.0	20.3	14.9	24.5	35.0
301-400	20.1	18.1	27.7	25.8	34.4	50.7
401-500	17.2	20.9	13.6	15.2	22.6	35.7
500 et plus	28.9	37.5	36.7	38.0	40.6	64.0
Total	241.0	231.6	346.0	300.6	298.2	438.1

Basis: Billion tonne-kms

Distance bracket (km)	Inland waterways 1980	Inland waterways 1990	Rail 1980	Rail 1990	Long-distance road transport 1980	Long-distance road transport 1990
0-50	0.9	0.7	2.9	1.8	0.4	0.6
51-100	5.0	4.7	3.0	2.8	2.9	4.2
101-150	3.9	3.5	3.5	2.8	6.9	9.8
151-200	4.1	3.6	3.8	3.4	7.7	10.6
201-250	3.1	2.7	4.9	4.1	6.8	9.5
251-300	2.8	2.2	5.6	4.2	6.8	9.7
301-400	7.1	6.5	9.6	8.9	12.0	17.6
401-500	7.6	9.2	6.1	6.6	10.1	16.0
500 et plus	16.9	21.7	24.2	26.1	26.7	42.5
Total	51.4	54.8	63.6	60.7	80.3	120.5

% shares by distance bracket

Basis: Goods carried in million tonnes

Distance bracket (km)	Inland waterways 1980	Inland waterways 1990	Rail 1980	Rail 1990	Long-distance road haulage 1980	Long-distance road haulage 1990
0-50	13.4	11.7	39.0	35.3	3.8	3.8
51-100	26.6	25.7	11.8	12.5	12.2	12.5
101-150	12.8	12.2	8.2	8.2	18.1	17.8
151-200	9.8	8.7	6.3	6.5	14.9	13.9
201-250	5.7	5.3	6.3	6.4	10.1	9.7
251-300	4.3	3.5	5.9	5.0	8.2	8.0
301-400	8.3	7.8	8.0	8.6	11.5	11.6
401-500	7.1	9.0	3.9	5.1	7.6	8.1
500 et plus	12.0	16.2	10.6	12.6	13.6	14.6
Total	100.0	100.0	100.0	100.0	100.0	100.0

Basis: Billion tonne-kms

Distance bracket (km)	Inland waterways 1980	Inland waterways 1990	Rail 1980	Rail 1990	Long-distance road transport 1980	Long-distance road transport 1990
0-50	1.8	1.3	4.6	3.0	0.5	0.5
51-100	9.7	8.6	4.7	4.6	3.6	3.5
101-150	7.6	6.4	5.5	4.6	8.6	8.1
151-200	8.0	6.6	6.0	5.6	9.6	8.8
201-250	6.0	4.9	7.7	6.8	8.5	7.9
251-300	5.4	4.0	8.8	6.9	8.5	8.0
301-400	13.8	11.9	15.1	14.7	14.9	14.6
401-500	14.8	16.8	9.6	10.9	12.6	13.3
500 et plus	32.9	39.6	38.1	43.0	33.3	35.3
Total	100.0	100.0	100.0	100.0	100.0	100.0

Annex 2. Gross value added by sector (%)

	1950	1960	1970	1980	1990	1993
Agriculture and forestry	**11.3**	**6.4**	**3.8**	**2.5**	**1.8**	**1.3**
Manufacturing sectors	**53.6**	**58.4**	**58.2**	**51.5**	**46.3**	**41.1**
Mining and energy	6.0	5.7	4.0	4.0	3.5	3.2
Energy and water supplies	1.8	2.6	2.5	3.0	2.9	2.7
Mining	4.2	3.0	1.4	1.0	0.6	0.5
Processing sectors	41.5	44.2	45.3	39.3	36.5	31.5
Chemicals	4.4	4.0	4.1	3.4	3.5	2.9
Mineral oil processing	0.0	1.4	1.9	2.2	1.4	1.7
Plastics and rubber	0.0	1.0	1.4	1.4	1.6	1.4
Stone and earth, ceramics, glass	2.2	2.4	2.3	1.8	1.4	1.4
Iron and non-ferrous ores and processing	2.8	5.9	4.4	3.1	2.7	1.9
Machinery and vehicles	6.1	8.4	10.9	10.6	10.7	8.6
Electrical and precision engineering, hardware/tinware	5.4	6.1	7.3	7.0	7.2	6.2
Woodworking and paper industry	4.8	3.5	3.6	3.1	2.8	2.7
Leather	-	0.8	0.5	0.3	0.2	0.1
Textiles	4.1	2.5	1.9	1.0	0.7	0.5
Clothing	2.7	1.2	1.2	0.7	0.5	0.4
Foodstuffs	9.1	3.6	2.9	2.6	2.2	2.1
Beverages	0.0	1.8	1.6	0.9	0.7	0.7
Tobacco	0.0	1.7	1.3	1.0	0.9	0.8
Construction	6.1	8.5	9.0	8.2	6.3	6.4
Trade and transport	**22.4**	**20.3**	**18.0**	**18.0**	**17.1**	**16.9**
Trade	14.5	13.2	11.4	11.0	10.5	10.4
Transport and communications	7.9	7.1	6.6	7.0	6.6	6.5
Services	**12.6**	**14.9**	**20.0**	**27.9**	**34.9**	**40.7**
Banking and insurance	2.7	2.6	3.8	5.5	5.7	7.0
Accommodation rentals	3.2	4.4	5.9	7.4	8.5	9.3
Other services	6.8	7.9	10.3	15.0	20.6	24.4
Total	**100.0**	**100.0**	**100.0**	**100.0**	**100.0**	**100.0**

Source: Data based on Federal Statistical Office yearbooks for various years.

BIBLIOGRAPHY

Arnold-Rothmaier, Hildegard (1996), "Aktuelle Tendenzen und Perspektiven in der Binnenschiffahrt", in: *Ifo-Schnelldienst*, No. 14.

Breitzmann, Karl-Heinz *et al.* (1993), "Containerlinienschiffahrt. Strukturen und Perspektiven des seewärtigen Containerverkehrs aus technisch-technologischer, organisatorisch-informationeller, wirtschaftlicher und kommerziell-rechtlicher Sicht", *Rostocker Beiträge zur Verkehrswissenschaft und Logistik*, Universität Rootstock.

ECMT (1990), *Inland Waterway Transport in ECMT Countries to the Year 2000: A new dimension*, Paris.

Eichler, Peter (1964), "Beschaffungslogistik für die größte Baustelle Europas", in: *11. Deutscher Logistik-Kongreß 1994, Band 2*, Münich, pp. 620-646.

Gudehus, T. (1995), "Die Lücke zwischen Schein und Sein, Auswahl Systemdienstleister", Serie, Teil 1, in: *Logistik Heute*, 1/2-1995, pp. 28-29.

Horyna, Karel (1996), "'Elbe-Labe-Container-Linie' als praktisches Beispiel für die Ost-West Zusammenarbeit", in: *Fluß-See-Schiffahrt in Europa -- Risiken und Chancen für den Ausbau kombinierter Verkehrssystem im Ost-West-Verkehr, 1. Europäisches Verkehrsforum*, Berlin.

IVB -- Ingenieurgesellschaft Verkehr Berlin (1995), "Wirtschaftliche Ausbaubedingungen für die Binnen- und Küstenschiffahrt im Wasserstraßendreieck Berlin-Eisenhüttenstadt-Schwedt/Szczecin", *Teil III: Zusammenfassung der deutschen und polnischen Untersuchungen*, Berlin.

Kalender, Ural (1993), "Stand der Hafenkonzepte in Berlin", in: *2. TUB/DVWG-Workshop: Binnenschiffahrt im Aufbruch -- Stand und Entwicklungen*, ISM-Bericht 93/9, Berlin.

Kieserling, Kornelia (1996), "Integration der Binnenschiffahrt in Just-in-Time Konzepte?", in: *Internationales Verkehrswesen* (48) 10/96, pp. 34-39.

Kirchoff, Bernd (1964), "Erdumschlag Potsdamer Platz, Vermarktung -- Verwertung – Verbringung", in: *11. Deutscher Logistik-Kongreβ 1994, Band 2*, München, pp. 648-666.

Linde, Horst/Teβmann, Günter (1995), "Hat die Binnenschiffahrt in der Oder-Region eine Zukunft?", in: *Internationales Verkehrswesen,* 47(1995)3, pp. 123-129.

Linde, Horst (1996), "Chances for operational combination of coastal and inland shipping in the Baltic area", International East/West Shipping Conference, Helsinki.
Linde, Horst (1995), "Die Wettbewerbsperspektiven der Binnenschiffahrt durch operative Verknüpfung von Binnen- und Küstenschiffahrt", in: *4. TUB/DVWG-Workshop: Die aktuelle Wettbewerbssituation der Binnenschiffahrt in einem liberalisierten europäischen Verkehrsmarkt*, ISM-Bericht 95/11, Berlin.

Lüüs, Hans-Peter (1996), "Binnenschiffahrt 1995", in: *Wirtschaft und Statistik*, No. 8/1996, pp. 507-513.

Maier, Wilhelm (1964), "Groβbaustelle Potsdamer Platz", in: *11. Deutscher Logistik-Kongreβ 1994, Band 2,* München, pp. 592-603.

Schönknecht, Rolf (1992), "Zukünftige Gütermärke der Binnenschiffahrt und resultierende transporttechnische und transportökonomische Anforderungen an die Binnenschiffahrt", in: *TUB/DVWG-Workshop: Perspektiven der Binnenschiffahrt im multimodalen Transportverbund der Zukunft*, ISM-Bericht 92/5, Berlin.

Stomberg, Heinrich (1995), "Entwicklung der europäischen Fluβ-/Seeschiffahrt", in: *3. TUB/DVWG-Workshop "Perspektiven der Schiffahrt in der Oder/Spree/Havel-Region"*, ISM-Bericht 95/3, Berlin.

Teßmann, Günter (1995), "Die Wettbewerbsfähigkeit der Binnenschiffahrt im Wasserstraßendreieck Berlin/Eisenhüttenstadt/Schwedt", in: *4. TUB/DVWG-Workshop: Die aktuelle Wettbewerbssituation der Binnenschiffahrt in einem liberalisierten europäischen Verkehrsmarkt,* ISM-Bericht 95/11, Berlin.

Voigt, Fritz (1973), *Verkehr, Erster Band: Die Theorie der Verkehrswirtschaft,* Berlin.

Von Stackelberg, Friedrich (1995), "Die Wettbewerbssituation der Binnenschiffahrt gegenüber den anderen Verkehrsträgern", in: *4. TUB/DVWG-Workshop: Die aktuelle Wettbewerbssituation der Binnenschiffahrt in einem liberalisierten europäischen Verkehrsmarkt,* ISM-Bericht 95/11, Berlin.

Walther, Michael (1995), "Stärkere Nutzung der Binnenschiffahrt -- Anspruch und Wirklichkeit einer aktiven Verkehrspolitik", in: *Internationales Verkehrswesen* 47(1995)9, pp. 528-534.

Wegener, Klaus-Günter (1996), "Die Vorteile des Fluß-See-Verkehrs für den europäischen Verlader", in: *Fluß-See-Schiffahrt in Europa -- Risiken und Chancen für den Ausbau kombinierter Verkehrssystem im Ost-West Verkehr, 1. Europäisches Verkehrsforum.* Berlin.

Zimmermann, Claus (1996), "Perspektiven im Containerverkehr", in: *Zeitschrift für Binnenschiffahrt*, No. 13.

Other sources:

BDB -- Bundesverband der Deutschen Binnenschiffahrt e.V., Geschäftsberichte;
BDB -- *Binnenschiffahrt in Zahlen*;
BÖB -- Bundesverband Öffentlicher Binnenhäfen e.V., Geschäftsberichte
Bundesverkehrsministerium: *Verkehr in Zahlen,* various years;
DVZ -- *Deutsche Verkehrszeitung;*
IVW -- *Internationales Verkehrswesen*;
Statistisches Bundesamt: *Statistisches Jahrbuch,* various years;
Statistisches Jahrbuch der DDR 1989, Berlin 1990;
ZfB -- *Zeitschfrift für Binnenschiffahrt.*

BELGIUM

Chris PEETERS
University of Antwerp (RUCA) and
Policy Research Corporation N.V.

Harry WEBERS
Policy Research Corporation N.V.
Antwerp
Belgium

ACKNOWLEDGEMENT

The authors would like to thank Drs. Antoon Soete, (Policy Research Corporation N.V. and Katholieke Universiteit Leuven (Center for Economic Studies) for useful suggestions and comments on an earlier draft of this paper.

THE IMPACT OF LIBERALISATION

SUMMARY

Antwerp, April 1997

53

1. INTRODUCTION

In the year 2000, the inland shipping sector will be liberalised as a means to achieve a really internal European market without boundaries.

In the year 2000, the inland shipping market in Europe will be liberalised. In accordance with the goal of achieving a really internal European market without boundaries (*Europe 1992*), the creation of one common market for transport via inland waterways is by now one of the remaining issues. The discussion on market regulation of the inland shipping sector started essentially when Germany abolished its system of *Festtariffe* as from 1st January 1994, without consulting the other Member States. The abolishment of this settlement caused serious problems in this sector, which made Germany decide to fight the market regulation in other European countries.

The liberalisation of transport by inland waterway does not apply to the River Rhine traffic, because this had already been liberalised since the Act of Mannheim.

Because on the River Rhine (and its side rivers) transport has been liberalised for many years (Act of Mannheim), liberalisation of transport via inland waterways thus only refers to the other waterways falling within the EC legislation on inland navigation, such as national waterways in Belgium, France, Germany and the Netherlands.

Essentially, there are two reasons why liberalisation of the inland shipping sector took such a long time, namely:

– the largest part of the inland shipping market (Rhine) had been liberalised a long time ago (Act of Mannheim);
– the structure of (the remaining part of) the inland shipping sector, being characterised by

relatively many independent small-scale firms, which caused national governments to pursue a strong regulatory policy.

Eventually, the liberalisation process will lead to the closing down of the current *alternating turn system (tour de rôle)*, originally designed to take care of a proportionate freight distribution at regulated prices, in order to achieve a uniform system which allows for free pricing and free contracting.

This means that, in the year 2000, a global European market will be created where prices are determined purely from supply and demand conditions. The part of the market which is currently organised via an alternating turn system will therefore be opened to allow for competition. The major objective of this paper is to discuss the economic consequences of such a change, though other aspects of liberalisation will be addressed too.

The focus of this paper is on pricing and capacity aspects related to the change from a regulated market towards a liberalised market.

In this paper, the focus is merely on *pricing* and *capacity* aspects which are related to the change from a regulated market towards a liberalised market.

On the one hand, prices in a liberalised market will be determined completely by the market forces and hence will show stronger fluctuations than in the past. In periods of off-peak demand, there is strong competition and prices will be relatively low, whereas in periods of peak demand, prices will be relatively high[1]. It is clear that price uncertainty is greater in a highly volatile market.

On the other hand, in the case of overcapacity, liberalisation will typically lead to a capacity reduction. Although, from an economic point of view, it is optimal to reduce the size of unused capacity, there is the danger of a growing discrepancy between short-term and long-term capacity requirements.

However, private initiatives such as partnership (in order to reduce risk and to increase flexibility) are possible means to overcome this problem and hence government intervention in this matter is not needed.

In the short run, price is the main instrument to equalise demand and supply. Therefore, the analysis starts with price competition in the context of rigid cost structures and product characteristics. In the long run, cost structures and product characteristics can be altered, either together or separately. For example, capacity may be adjusted or product characteristics may be changed. These instruments will also be analysed in more detail.

Furthermore, the abrogation of the restrictive settlements with respect to chartering and pricing are expected to have a most positive effect on transport by inland waterways. This will also be discussed in more detail.

Throughout this paper, the Belgian situation will be used frequently as a case study in order to illustrate and evaluate the specific problems and policy measures.

As the perspective of the paper is rather broad, the arguments made are applicable to all EU Member countries. To illustrate and evaluate the specific problems and policy measures, however, the Belgian situation is most often referred to [see also Peeters (1992)].

The paper is organised as follows. In Chapter 2, the factors in favour of or militating against the alternating turn system are discussed. In Chapter 3, the trade-off between the stabilizing effect originated by artificial price rigidities (as in the alternating turn system) and the competitive effect inherent to free-market pricing (as in the liberalised system) is analysed. Chapter 4 focuses on the determination of a realistic level of excess capacity, whereas in Chapter 5 different means to remove the abundant excess supply are discussed in more detail. In Chapter 6 the regulatory measures taken by the European Community and the Belgian Government are put into perspective. Chapter 7 concludes.

2. THE IMAGE OF INLAND SHIPPING

In Belgium, the inland shipping sector has a negative image.

The image of inland shipping differs greatly among the EU Member States. In the Netherlands, for example, the sector has adjusted reasonably well to the changing market conditions over the last decade. As such, scrap-and-build campaigns were used to greatly renew the shipping fleet. In Belgium, the situation is worse: the sector is badly organised and a large part of the inland shipping fleet is old, because only scrapping campaigns were effectively executed.

Hence, the inland shipping sector in Belgium has a negative image which is being paralysed by the alternating turn system. It should be noted, however, that only part of the transport by inland waterways is regulated via the alternating turn system[2]. This system has led to overcapacity, a lack of investments and an unsympathetic attitude towards (potential) customers. In Belgium, however, the size of the overcapacity is relatively small, because of the absence of large building campaigns.

The process of liberalisation and the measures taken to support this change are focused on:

– improving the infra- and superstructure;
– assisting those who are willing to stay in the profession;
– assisting those who are willing to give up their profession.

Measures taken to assure a greater flexibility and a better quality may help to optimally exploit the well-equipped network of inland waterways.

With these measures, it is possible to create a greater flexibility and a better quality. It should be noted, however, that the third measure, assisting those who are willing to stop the profession, has been applied relatively unsuccessfully many times before. Therefore, the other measures should deserve much greater attention. Currently, the existing regulations and the obligatory Sunday rest for the inland shipping sector oppose an optimal development of the Belgian inland shipping sector. Nevertheless, the network of inland waterways in Belgium is one of the best equipped in Europe, which certainly has great potential[3].

2.1. The alternating turn system in Belgium

The economic depression in the thirties caused many problems in the inland shipping sector. Government intervention in the market functioning was needed to overcome these problems. Ship loading via the alternating turn system was, in the first instance, intended for domestic goods transport. Later, transport to France was added and for transport to the Netherlands an announcement duty was put into operation. Since the strikes of the inland shippers in the early seventies, however, an unofficial alternating turn system for transport to the Netherlands has prevailed. In the alternating turn system, prices and freight conditions are being fixed. Although there never was an alternating turn system for the tanker trade, minimum prices have been in use since 1981 for this type of transport.

2.2. Factors in favour of the alternating turn system

The existence of regulatory mechanisms (such as the alternating turn system) can partly be explained by the existence of imperfections in the market for transport by inland waterways.

From an economic point of view, the market for transport by inland waterways has certain imperfections that (to some extent) favour the existence of a regulatory mechanism, such as the alternating turn system. The market imperfections frequently mentioned are the following:

– Demand for transport by inland waterways is difficult to influence by the sector as a whole;
– Low transparency of market conditions;
– Fluctuating capacity requirements (the existence of peak-load capacity negatively influences prices in off-peak periods);
– Because of round trips, lower prices may be offered.

In particular, the fluctuating capacity requirements are cumbersome for the inland shipping sector because investments in ships are high and long term. Also, at low water, additional capacity is required because, in that instance, ships can be loaded less heavily.

In recent years, many small ships have been scrapped due to a new scrap campaign. Consequently, an important part of the spare capacity has disappeared, which may cause capacity restrictions in periods of peak demand. Therefore, prices are likely to show more variation in the near future[4]. Together with the abolition of the current alternating turn system, its stabilizing feature will disappear.

The industrial structure of the inland shipping sector, being characterised by many small-scale firms, causes additional problems, which favour the existence of a regulatory mechanism. In Belgium, for example, no fewer than 90 per cent of the total number of organisations in the inland shipping sector are one-ship firms. It is not surprising, therefore, that advocates of the alternating turn system are found mainly among the small, independent skippers.

2.3. Factors militating against the alternating turn system

The main disadvantage of the alternating turn system is that it may create the wrong or too few incentives (inefficiencies, etc.).

Closing down the alternating turn system will lead to a larger dynamism in the sector and, as such, may prove a useful tool to create the right incentives for carriers (long-term commitments, specialisation, investment). In the liberalisation process, quality and service are becoming more important aspects, which is expected to improve the competitive strength of inland shipping compared to other transport alternatives.

One of the negative aspects of the alternating turn system is that there is no long-term relationship between principals and carriers. Such relationships could provide more economically efficient transport, because, for example, ships need not be cleaned after use and residual waste will no longer be drained off. Furthermore, economies of scale can be achieved by organising transport via long-term relationships.

Also in a liberalised market, specialisation in certain transport modes is likely to occur. Furthermore, in such a situation, there is the possibility for skippers and freight forwarders to sign contracts in order to offer multimodal transport. Whenever the inland shipping sector is able to offer such a global transport package at a competitive price (through cost reduction of transport or transhipment), a strong increase in traffic is to be expected.

3. MARKET STRUCTURE AND PRICING

In this chapter, a methodological approach is presented to describe the structure and functioning of the market for transport by inland waterways.

The market for transport by inland waterways is composed of a large number of small carriers and a small number of large shipping companies.

The *demand* for transport services is exercised by a relatively small number of (large) companies, whereas the *supply* side is characterised by a relatively large number of (small) firms. In the economics literature, this market may typically be classified as an oligopolistic type of market (*oligopsony*). In such a market, the demand side has some market power over the supply side, which in a *free market* would enable them to obtain particularly competitive rates from the suppliers[5].

However, in a market regulated through price restrictions (for example, via an alternating turn system), there are fewer possibilities for the demand side to exercise its market power. In that respect, competition on the supply side is relaxed, which in turn yields higher prices for the demand side (the shippers)[6].

The situations with and without price restrictions are depicted in Figures 1 and 2 and respectively. In these figures, supply (*S*) and demand (*D*) for transport as a function of the price *p* are (for ease of convenience) according to the linear specifications $S(p)=p$ and $D(p)=1-1.5*p$, so supply is increasing in price and demand is decreasing in price[7]. It is easily checked that, in a free market, supply and demand equalise at a price of *0.4*. However, it will be assumed that, due to an alternating turn system, prices are bound below at 0.5, which creates a situation of excess supply.

In such a case of price rigidities, price competition will only be softened as long as this minimum price level is *above* the free market price. This is the situation depicted in Figure 1. When the minimum price level is *below* the free market price, the price restriction is ineffective, and hence essentially a free market system is at stake (see Figure 2).

Excess supply exists at the expense of a higher price.

In the situation depicted in Figure 1, there is an excess supply at the minimum price level. At this price, the demand for transport by inland waterways is below the free market level (so firms use other transport alternatives relatively more) and the supply is above the free market level. Because of the excess supply, it is possible to easily absorb demand fluctuations without affecting the price (see dotted line). Nevertheless, this is at the expense of a price higher than the free market level.

Figure 1. **Demand and supply under a regime of minimum pricing (as in the alternating turn system)**

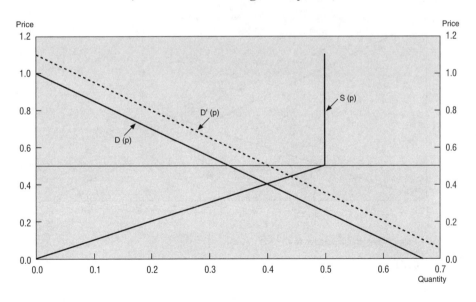

Source: Policy Research Corporation N.V.

The free market case, i.e. the situation without price restrictions, is depicted in Figure 2. Here, the price is determined completely by demand and supply factors. Consequently, a higher demand will automatically lead to higher prices. Only if there is idle ship capacity available will supply increase. However, if (short-term) capacity is restricted to the free-market level, supply cannot change and hence the price will rise even faster.

Also in a dynamic perspective, the imbalance between supply and demand causes problems. Because of the long construction time of ships, investment decisions taken in periods of peak demand may yield excess supply once they can be put into use.

Figure 2. **Demand and supply under a free pricing regime**

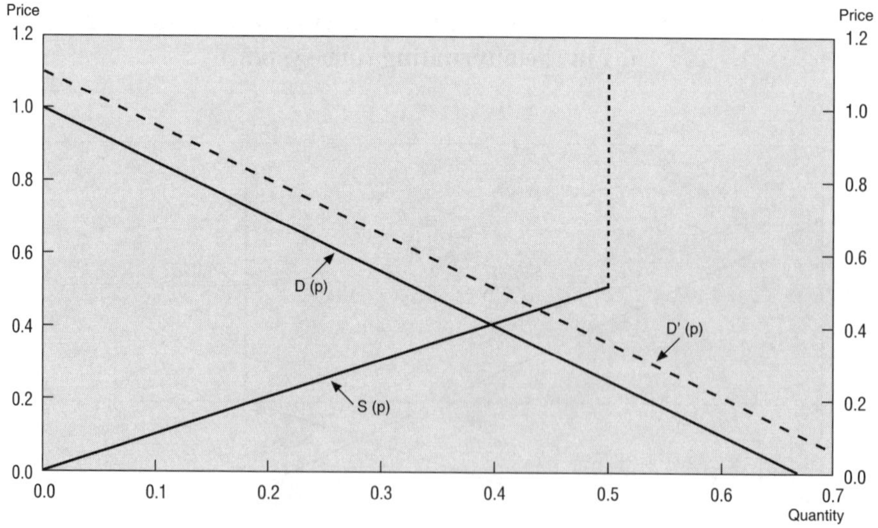

Source: Policy Research Corporation N.V.

The two main problems concerning market liberalisation are:
- *fluctuating prices (which are lower in off-peak periods, but may be higher in peak periods);*
- *absence of excess supply (to offer enough capacity in peak periods).*

From Figure 1 and 2, the two main problems concerning market liberalisation can be identified:

- (initially) free market prices are lower than restricted prices but, principally, prices are no longer fixed because they are inherent to changes in demand and supply;
- the excess supply in case of price restrictions is no longer present in a free market.

If, ideally, demand would not change over time, the free market solution is the optimal one. In that case, prices are lower and excess supply (although not available) is not required. However, if demand *fluctuates* over time, the absence of excess supply may cause problems. First, in the short run, there is a sharp price increase in order to equalise demand and supply (and hence there is an increased use of alternative transport *modi*). Second, in the long run the shortage of supply may be followed by an increase in supply (through putting new ships into use).

The stabilizing feature inherent to price restrictions has advantages for both the demand and the supply side. First, prices are fixed and well known in advance. Second, the availability of excess supply is important to ensure the short-term reliability and flexibility (and to prevent frequent changes to other transport alternatives such as rail and road).

From a social point of view, it is optimal that the positive aspects of both the current alternating turn system and the free market system are integrated.

Nevertheless, there are also disadvantages with respect to such price restrictions. For the demand side, a much oversized excess supply is not desirable, because this will never be used but it has to be paid for via high prices. For the supply side as a whole, oversized excess supply only means a cost without yielding additional revenues. Consequently, it is to the interest of all parties that the positive aspects of both the current alternating turn system (with price rigidities) and the free market system are integrated.

The goal of liberalisation should be on reduction of excess supply towards a level which is required in peak periods. Such peak-pricing ensures:

— a more realistic and constant price (at a level somewhere between the free-market price and the initial restricted price);
— a realistic excess supply.

Liberalisation, in the sense of achieving a free market situation, therefore, should not be a goal in itself. The objective of liberalisation should be more on reduction of excess supply (i.e. a relative increase of demand) towards a level which is required for in peak periods. Such peak-pricing ensures:

- a more realistic and constant price (at a level somewhere between the free market price and the initial restricted price);
- a realistic excess supply.

Perhaps the most important advantage of such a system is the fact that shippers and carriers will (need to) become connected more closely, which in its turn increases the transparency of the market and simplifies the contracting between shippers and carriers.

However, it is clear that shippers (rightly) are only willing to pay for excess capacity as far as they (expect to) need it. Although the determination of such a realistic level may be difficult beforehand, in a free market this is what finally will result. In this respect, pricing negotiations between suppliers and demanders for transport by inland waterways will provide this market clearance function and hence may play an important role.

4. A REALISTIC LEVEL OF EXCESS SUPPLY

By now, it is generally believed that the market for transport by inland waterways as a whole is characterised by a shortage of demand or a relative abundance of capacity.

Essentially, this means that, currently, part of the capacity is not needed, not even in peak periods. This abundant capacity is implicitly paid for by shippers via the *mark-up on prices*, whereas it does not yield returns. In case of liberalisation, increased competition would remove this capacity. It is obvious that the demand side benefits from a lowering of the price. But, more importantly, the suppliers could also benefit by removing abundant capacity, because this will positively affect demand and reduce costs (*inter alia* by an increased utilisation of the remaining capacity). From a *normative* point of view, it can be derived that a reduction of abundant capacity is socially optimal, because in fact it simply means a reduction in costs.

This is illustrated by the example described in the previous chapter, with demand and supply being given by $S(p)=p$ and $D(p)=1-1.5*p$. With a cost per unit capacity of 0.1, the results obtained are gathered in Table 1.

Table 1. **Comparison of price, demand and supply in a regulated market and a free market**

Situation	price	demand	supply	cost of capacity	gross revenue for suppliers	net revennue for suppliers
regulated market	0.5	0.25	0.5	0.05	0.125	0.075
free-market	0.4	0.4	0.4	0.04	0.16	0.12

Source: Policy Research Corporation N.V.

From this table, it is easily seen that the removal of price constraints will lead to a lower price at which excess supply is zero. Consequently, the cost of supply is reduced. In this example furthermore, there is a strong positive demand effect (due to a large price elasticity). Because of the cost decrease and the strong demand increase, the net revenue for the suppliers will rise[8].

The reduction of abundant capacity is socially optimal because the capacity cost is then decreased. Possible effects on the price level do not matter from a social point of view, because this is just a monetary transfer from the demand to the supply side.

Since the price paid for transport is just a monetary transfer from the demand side to the supply side, a reduction of abundant capacity is socially optimal.

Liberalisation will result in a lower price and reduce the current abundance of excess supply. As was argued before, it may nevertheless be beneficial to maintain some excess capacity, because of the fluctuation of demand over time [either in a seasonal manner or over the business cycle: see, for example, Arrow, Beckmann and Karlin (1958)][9].

Three possible ways to overcome the relative abundance of excess supply are:
– *an upward shift of long-term demand curve (demand increase);*
– *an upward shift of long-term supply curve (supply decrease);*
– *abolishment or a downward shift of the regulated price.*

Basically, there are three ways to overcome the relative abundance of excess supply, namely:

– an upward shift of long-term demand curve (demand increase);

– an upward shift of long-term supply curve (supply decrease);

– abolishment or a downward shift of the regulated (rigid) price.

Stimulation of demand should be used more frequently as a means to reduce the relative abundance of excess supply. The main focus of politicians, unfortunately, is still on scrapping up capacity, although in the past this has proved to be relatively unsuccessful.

Liberalisation, in principle, refers directly to the last of these measures, but the same impact can be reached by the other two measures. These two measures will be discussed more extensively in the next section, because meanwhile they are taken as temporary measures by the individual countries to prepare for full liberalisation in the year 2000. The stimulation of demand, as pointed out in the first measure, is most important and promising and hence justifies strong efforts in a broad marketing of transport via inland waterways. Unfortunately, by now, demolition as a means to reduce the supply still receives the most attention from decisionmakers.

It should be clear that each of these measures is a step towards liberalisation, so pricing will be based more on demand and supply factors. With an appropriate mix of these measures, it is possible to achieve a level of excess capacity which ensures supply in periods of peak load. Because of the changes in demand and supply over time, in a liberalised market as well this "realistic" level of excess supply will show variations over time.

5. WAYS TO REDUCE EXCESS CAPACITY

As was mentioned earlier, an increase of demand or a decrease of supply are both means to reduce excess capacity. Therefore, they may be useful tools in order to achieve a liberalised market (without price regulations). In the past, attention was given purely to the scrapping up of capacity, albeit with little success. The stimulation of demand, on the other hand, is much more promising and finally should get the attention it deserves[10].

5.1. Stimulation of demand for transport via inland waterways

Stimulation of demand for transport via inland waterways requires a broad transport policy which recognises the importance of anti-pollution and congestion-reducing transport alternatives, such as inland shipping.

Such a broad framework on transport and mobility should be carried out by the European Union and its Member States, which is presently still in its infancy. With the lack of such a rudimentary basis, actions to stimulate transport by inland waterways are difficult to design and co-ordinate. Therefore, the design of a common transport and mobility framework requires considerable attention.

The actions taken by the Belgian Government in order to attract more traffic on inland waterways are the following. In section 6.2., the specific transitional actions taken by the Walloon and Flemish governments are presented. For a more extensive description of the background for the Flemish measures, see Policy Research Corporation N.V. (1990, 1993, 1995-1996).

First, there is the provision of investments for modernisation and technological adaptation. *Second*, as a means to attract non-traditional traffic, subsidies are given to companies which invest in the construction of inland terminals. *Third*, the size-up of firms is stimulated by subsidising the purchase of secondhand ships. *Fourth*, there are contributions to the co-operation between individual skippers and shippers. *Fifth*, education and other quality-improving actions are stimulated.

The co-operation between individual skippers and shippers should create a buffer in order to provide a secure and professional cargo handling. Also, the

70

provision of additional logistic functions, such as planning of transport, guarantee of large contracts and combined selling power, will yield advantages.

Perhaps the most important element is the change in attitude of (a part of) the sector. In particular, when the liberalisation process has settled down, the sector should be exploiting commercial activities. Then the sector itself should search actively for clients. From several studies on inland shipping conducted by *Policy Research Corporation N.V.,* it may be concluded that such commercial activities are crucial in the actual promotion of inland shipping [see, for example, Policy Research Corporation N.V. (1993, 1996-1997)].

In order to determine the real potential for inland shipping, more in-depth studies are required which look at the price elasticity of demand for transport by inland waterways.

In order to determine the real potential for inland shipping, the execution of more in-depth studies is needed, in which the price elasticity of demand for transport by inland shipping is determined. Because the price (for the whole transport trajectory) is by far the most important choice factor with respect to inland shipping, it should finally get the attention it deserves. Beforehand, the uncertainties with respect to the (EU) regulations on mobility and the regulations concerning the different transport alternatives should be taken away.

Anyhow, a traffic increase requires actions on a micro-economic level to induce or stimulate firms to use inland shipping (more frequently) as a means of transport.

5.2. Ways to reduce the level of excess supply

In order to reduce the overcapacity in the inland shipping market, the European Commission has allowed:

–   the provision of national subsidies to support certain investments in infrastructure alongside inland waterways:
–   the co-financing by the European Union of the scrapping of ships.

As already mentioned earlier, the fluctuation of demand over time is one of the major reasons to hold access supply.   Therefore, all measures which enhance the stability of demand will reduce the cost of holding idle capacity.

Because of the possibility of *risk diversification*, co-operation between carriers or the concentration of carriers, for example, are important means to reduce excess capacity[11].   Furthermore, co-operation between carriers strengthens their market position in relation to the shippers and offers many possibilities to provide a better service.

Also, long-term commitments between shippers and carriers may be used in order to reduce demand uncertainty.   Typically, tonnage and price could be negotiated and laid down in a written contract, but contracting of prices will be less commonly used (because shippers usually keep the option of using alternative transport *modi*).   Such *contracting* reduces risk and uncertainty for both parties.

Unfortunately, in practice, contracts are fairly incomplete, owing to *transaction costs*.   According to Coase (1937) and Williamson (1975), four types of transaction costs can be distinguished, two of which occur at the contracting date and two of which occur later.

First, some contingencies which the parties will face may not be foreseeable at the contracting date. Second, even if they could be foreseen, there may be too many contingencies to write into the contract. Third, monitoring the contract may be costly. Fourth, enforcing contracts (when necessary) may involve considerable costs.

Besides the reduction of demand uncertainty, contracting will also prove to be very useful in order to offer better quality and service.

5.3. Scrapping campaigns

Due to the latest scrapping campaigns in certain categories of ships, shortages have appeared.

Due to the latest scrapping campaigns, shortages have appeared in certain categories of ships. In order to effectively stimulate the transport via inland waterways, the focus should be on differentiation of capacity rather than on size. Also for small ships, which are able to travel low-profile canals, there is a *raison d'être*. The course of action should be on break-up of ships of different types and tonnage, rather than on break-up of ships simply after announcement.

6. DIRECTIVE OF THE EUROPEAN COMMISSION

In the early nineties, the discussion on liberalisation of the inland shipping sector was initiated by the European Commission. From then on, it took several years before the European Commission promulgated a Directive to the Member States. This Directive provides for a gradual liberalisation of the inland shipping sector (with free pricing and free contracting). As from 1st January 2000, the liberalisation should be completed and, until that time, Member States have the possibility to issue transitional regulations.

The Directive states, *inter alia*, that, after being put into operation, contracts concerning term and tonnage should be removed little by little from the alternating turn system. The transport of containers, private transport, transport of liquids, transport within sea harbours, transport with ships having their own discharge and load equipment, transport which cannot be cleared via the alternating turn system as well as multimodal transport, should come about freely.

6.1. Transitional regulations

The Directive of the European Commission allows Member States to take transitional measures to prepare their national inland shipping sector for the changing market conditions in the year 2000. In France, a gradual liberalisation is planned, and in the Netherlands the North-South Law provides many openings. In Belgium, until recently, all freight was subject to standard conditions determined by law. In certain sub-markets, even contract conditions were laid down. This regulatory task is still being executed by the DRB (*Dienst voor Regeling der Binnenvaart*)[12].

The main objective -- in the short run -- of the policy measures formulated by the Belgian Government is not the elimination of the alternating turn system but merely the change towards a more flexible system on pricing and

In order to meet the requirements of the Directive of the European Commission, the Belgian Government has formulated several resolutions. In these resolutions, the main objective is not the elimination of the alternating turn system but merely the change towards a more flexible system on pricing and contracting as well as the provision of better quality and service. However, none of these measures (the Verschueren Act) has yet been implemented.

contracting. But none of these measures (the Verschueren Act) has been implemented yet.

The measures taken by the Belgian Government are aimed at liberating the freights, leaving out growth markets from the alternating turn system, and at "free" pricing (via collective deliberation) and contracting[13].

The European Directive, however, is more comprehensive and is in conflict with the statute, the legal basis, of the DRB. This statute says that freight for transport by inland waterways should pass by the DRB, which conflicts with the Treaty of Rome on competition regulation. Therefore, the DRB must be dissolved or its task should be changed.

Because the policy measures have not yet been implemented, it is doubtful if transitional measures will ever be taken, because in the year 2000 the inland shipping market will be completely liberalised.

The existing alternating turn system in Belgium is comparable to the German system of *Festtariffe* in the past, and is therefore also in conflict with the provisions of the Treaty of Rome. Although the operation of an alternating turn system is prohibited for firms, it is allowed for governments because these serve a public interest. Juridically speaking, such regulations are permitted, but the political goal is the creation of a free market. In this context, the granting by the Belgian Government of the skippers' request to legalise the alternating turn system should be seen as a harmonization towards liberalisation[14].

6.2. Transitional measures taken by the Walloon and Flemish governments

The measures taken by the Walloon and Flemish governments will ease the change from a regulated market to a competitive market for the inland shipping sector.

Both the Walloon and Flemish governments have signed an agreement in principle with the European Commission concerning supporting measures regarding liberalisation of the inland shipping sector. These measures can, in fact, be seen as further specifications of the ones presented in section 5.1.

The Walloon Government has taken measures to ease the change from a regulated market to a competitive market for the inland shipping sector.

The three building blocks are:

– financial support for the development of commercial unions, in order to induce skippers to join a commercial structure which will be able to meet the requirements of a free market;
– subsidies on investments in technological adjustments;
– subsidies on investments in superstructure.

The Flemish Government has foreseen a budget of 1 billion BEF in order to:

– reduce capacity by scrapping old ships or ships that are no longer required by the market;
– subsidise (between 15 and 21 per cent) adjustment investments in inland ships;
– subsidise investments in infrastructure by private companies;
– subsidise educational initiatives and co-operation agreements between skippers;
– take social measures for the sector.

7. CONCLUSION

The liberalisation of the inland shipping sector certainly opens up new markets for transport by inland waterways. However, this requires a broad transport policy which recognises the importance of an environment- and congestion-friendly transport alternative. Until now, few actions have been taken in this respect. The Member States of the EU should give priority to the establishment of a uniform vision on transport and mobility policy and make choices in this respect. Only then can a shift towards a more dynamic sector, which is no longer being paralysed by the alternating turn system, yield an increased use of inland shipping.

To a large extent, such an increased use of inland shipping should come from microeconomic measures. In a liberalised market, individual firms will be able to offer the required tailor-made services the market is asking for.

On the other hand, it is needless to say that the liberalisation of the market should be carried out carefully. Because of the specific market structure, it is argued in this paper that liberalisation should focus on integration of the positive aspects of the current alternating turn system (its stabilizing feature) and the free-market system (its competitiveness). Due to the fluctuation of demand over time, it is optimal to maintain a certain level of excess capacity. However, this does not necessitate government intervention, because private initiatives are responding very well (or even better) to such changing conditions. The role of the government in this matter should be more on preparing the skippers to the changing market condition, for example, by stimulating partnerships and training.

NOTES

1. In the Belgian context, the prices charged under the alternating turn system are expected to be about 30 per cent above the free market price level.

2. In 1992, the total cargo (domestic plus transit) shipped via inland waterways in Belgium was about 92 million tons; 23 million tons were shipped via the alternating turn system. In this system, the traffic from and to France amounts to 4 million tons, whereas the traffic from and to the Netherlands amounts to 10 million tons. The remaining nine tons shipped via the alternating turn system are accounted for by the domestic transport of dry bulk. The alternating turn system includes, for example, building materials (such as sand and gravel). The cargo not shipped via the alternating turn system largely concerns the River Rhine traffic.

3. The combination of liberalisation and the addition of infrastructure could very well double the total traffic on inland waterways. However, by now, very little can be said about the price elasticity of demand, so research on this topic is certainly needed.

4. To some extent, this is an argument in favour of liberalisation, because then the real scarcity of production factors is measured. Both this free market argument and the stabilizing feature of price rigidities are important for the inland shipping sector.

5. For ease of exposition, no distinction is made between the different types of capacities supplied. Capacity here is seen as the total tonnage available. However, the analysis may also be applied to certain types of capacity.

6. It will be argued later that the existence of artificially high prices will lead to an abundance of excess capacity which, from a socioeconomic point of view, is inefficient.

7. In fact, supply and demand for transport by inland waterways is not only a function of own price, but also a function of the prices of competing transport *modi*. In the analysis, these prices are assumed to be fixed and hence they need not be mentioned separately.

8. In the case of small price elasticity, the demand effect is also smaller. The net revenue of the suppliers could well then be below the outcome under the regulated system. However, liberalisation is beneficial for the economy as a whole, which means that an "allocation mechanism" (agreement) could make both carriers and shippers better off.

9. If the supply side were more concentrated, there might also be other more strategic reasons for having excess capacity, for example, to fight aggressive pricing behaviour [see Maskin and Tirole (1985)].

10. In a recent marketing study by Policy Research for the Sea-Canal Corporation (N.V. Zeekanaal), a strategic plan was drawn up in which actions on a microeconomic level are the key to increasing transport by inland waterways [see Policy Research Corporation N.V. (1995-96)].

11. Such scaling up may, furthermore, yield cost reductions and may eventually lead to a less competitive market structure.

12. The DRB is an institution for the benefit of the community, which is under the control of the Ministry of Transport. Its receipts come mainly from the alternating turn system.

13. A general reference system of freight rates, prices and conditions will be drafted, which should be approved by the "Freight Committee". This is a committee of 18 people, consisting of nine shippers and nine freight forwarders and brokers. From each group of representatives, a majority must agree with these reference prices and conditions. Besides the determination of general modalities (not per individual contract) the Freight Committee also sets the contracting conditions on term and tonnage. The reference prices will not distinguish between different kinds of goods categories. It is foreseen that firms which operate more than twenty ships or which have a loading capacity of more than 50 000 tons, are allowed to charge up to 70 per cent of the DRB price. Therefore, it is likely that the new prices will be 30 per cent below the normal DRB level. Except for the traffic to and from France and the Netherlands, this is mostly the current market price.

14. Because it is just a formal tying up of the current situation, it does not imply a further competitive disadvantage for the regions concerned.

BIBLIOGRAPHY

Arrow, Beckmann, and Karlin (1958), "The optimal expansion of the capacity of a firm", in: *Arrow, Karlin, and Scarf.*

Coase (1937), "The nature of the firm", *Economica* No. 4, pp. 386-405.

Maskin and Tirole (1985), "A theory of dynamic oligopoly, II: Price Competition", MIT, Working Paper 373.

Peeters (1992), "De Belgische Scheepsbouw en Scheepvaart", Economische Analyse en Evaluatie van het overheidsbeleid, Deel I en II (Belgian Shipbuilding and Shipping. Economic Analysis and Evaluation of Government Policy, Parts I and II).

Policy Research Corporation N.V. (1990), "Evaluatie van de Economische Impact van de transportsector in Vlaanderen: de zeehavensector, de binnenvaartsector en de wegvervoersector", studie in opdracht van het Ministerie van de Vlaamse Gemeenschap (Evaluation of the economic impact of the transport sector in Flanders: the sea port sector, the inland navigation sector and the road haulage sector).

Policy Research Corporation N.V. (1993), "Onderzoek naar ondersteunings mechanismen voor de binnenvaart, alsmede overslaginfrastructuur", studie in opdracht van vzw Promotie Binnenvaart Vlaanderen (Development of policy measures to improve the competitive position of inland navigation).

Policy Research Corporation N.V. (1995-96), "Vergelijkend onderzoek van de concurrentiepositie van de Vlaamse Binnenvaartondernemers ten opzichte van de Nederlandse Binnenvaartondernemers", studie in opdracht van de vzw Promotie Binnenvaart Vlaanderen (uitgevoerd in samenwerking met Price Waterhouse, Plant Location International). [Analysis of the competitive position of the Flemish Inland Navigation Sector compared to the Inland Navigation Sector of the Netherlands (study conducted in co-operation with Price Waterhouse, Plant Location International)].

Policy Research Corporation N.V. (1996-97), "Marktpositionering en uitwerking van een marketingstrategie voor de N.V. Zeekanaal, studie in opdracht van de N.V. Zeekanaal". [Market study of the competitive position of the N.V. Zeekanaal and the subsequent marketing strategy (inland navigation and short sea shipping)].

Williamson (1975), *Markets and Hierarchies: Analysis and Anti-trust Implications*, New York, Free Press.

FRANCE

Marie-Madeleine DAMIEN
Professeur à l'Université de Lille 1
UFR de Géographie et d'Aménagement
Villeneuve d'Ascq

Chargé de Cours à l'Institut Universitaire de Technologie
Évry
France

SUMMARY

Evry, March 1997

1. WHAT IS THE CURRENT SITUATION WITH REGARD TO TRANSPORT BY INLAND WATERWAYS?

1.1. Trends in inland waterway traffic in Europe

1.1.1 Traffic within the European Union

Between 1970 and 1994, the inland transport sector within the European Union grew by a spectacular 66.3 per cent. During this period, the total annual volume of traffic rose from 890 to 1 490 billion t-km.

The modal split for freight traffic within the European Union shows that in absolute terms output increased in all modes except for rail, which experienced a sharp decline. The inland waterways ranked third after road, the largest mode, whose continued growth is cause for serious concern over the future of our environment (see Table 1).

Table 1. **Modal split for freight traffic within the European Union (15)**
(t-km millions)

	Road	Rail	Inland waterways	Pipeline	Total
1970	431	283	110	66	890
1975	526	259	103	79	969
1980	661	287	113	92	1 153
1985	711	275	103	71	1 161
1990	915	255	113	72	1 355
1993	964	205	106	82	1 358
1994	1 061*	220	115	83	1 479
1994-70	+146%	-22%	+5%	+25%	+66%

*   German statistics include the former GDR from 1994 onwards.
Sources: ECMT, UC, DW, national statistics.

The inland transport sector grew at an average annual rate of 2.1 per cent over the period 1970-94. The inland waterways sector, which ranked third in terms of share of the modal split, grew at an average annual rate of 0.1 per cent. The inland waterways thus outperformed the rail sector, whose output declined by 1.1 per cent; average annual growth in the road sector, however, amounted to 3.8 per cent.

The inland waterways also ranked third in the modal split in terms of relative value (Table 2).

Table 2. **Modal split (as a percentage)**

	Road	**Rail**	*Inland waterways*	**Pipeline**
1970	48.5	31.8	12.3	7.4
1975	54.4	26.8	10.7	8.2
1980	57.4	24.9	9.8	8.0
1985	61.2	23.7	8.9	6.1
1990	67.5	18.9	8.3	5.3
1994	71.7	14.9	7.8	5.6

The performance of the inland waterways in this respect needs to be seen in context, however, in that only six EU Member States have a fully operational inland waterway network: France, the Netherlands, Belgium, Luxembourg, Germany and Austria.

Table 3. **Trend in inland waterway traffic in countries with a fully operational waterway network**

	Length of waterway network (km)		**Waterway traffic (t-km billion)**		**Trend in traffic**
	1970	**1994**	**1970**	**1994**	**94-70 as %**
France	7 433	7 376	14.2	5.6	-61
Germany	4 508	6 958*	48.8	61.8**	+23
Netherlands	5 999	5 046	30.7	36.1	+18
Belgium	1 553	1 513	6.7	5.5	-18

*   After reunification.
**   Of which 2 billion t-km in the former GDR.
Source: Eurostat.

In 1995, the German inland waterway network carried 238 million tonnes of freight, an increase of 1.4 per cent compared with the previous year, and the average length of trips rose from 263 to 268 km. Waterway traffic in the Netherlands continued to rise, gaining market share from road. The waterways carried 97 million tonnes of domestic freight and 155 million tonnes of international freight, an increase of over 4 million tonnes on the previous year. Traffic levels were also up in France and amounted to 54.8 million tonnes in 1995.

Traffic levels on the inland waterways in the EU area are closely linked to those of the maritime ports through which the main traffic flows are channelled.

The inadequacy of inland waterway infrastructure in France explains the very low share of inland waterways in the modal split and the weak performance of French maritime ports, which in many cases have a limited hinterland. Fleets are hostages to their river basins. The collapse of inland waterway traffic in Belgium is partly the result of an outdated and overregulated commercial policy.

Table 4. **Comparison of maritime and inland waterway traffic levels in various European ports**

	Maritime traffic (mill. tonnes)	**Inland waterway traffic (tonne millions)**		**Waterway/maritime (as %)**
	1995	**1990**	**1995**	**1995**
Rotterdam	294	120	110	37
Antwerp	108	50	54	50
Hamburg	72.1		10.2	14
Le Havre	54	3.1	3.2	5.9
Dunkirk	39		1.7	4.3
Rouen	20	3	2.7	13.5
Marseilles	87	1.5	1.0	4.3

1.1.2   Traffic in central and eastern Europe

The figures for traffic in Europe as a whole, including Russia, Ukraine, the Baltic States and Belarus (Table 5a) reveal a dramatic decline in inland waterway traffic in eastern Europe.

The volume of traffic in this area fell from 756 million tonnes in 1988 to 284 million tonnes in 1993, a decline of 63 per cent. This decline was so severe that it resulted in an overall decline in worldwide inland waterway traffic (excluding China and South America). Traffic in western Europe, however, has remained relatively unaffected. A number of factors were responsible for the collapse of inland waterway traffic in eastern Europe, among which the end to the anti-economic practices associated with the planned economies in these countries and the abandoning of the barter trade that had developed between the socialist countries. Some countries, for example, had been forced to accept deliveries of coal and ore. These flows, which are estimated to have amounted to around 15 million tonnes, were primarily carried by inland waterway. The downsizing of certain fleets, including the Russian fleet, is also a factor in the decline in traffic levels. In many cases, Russian vessels have remained idle since the breakdown of the Soviet system. Originally manufactured in eastern European countries, former East Germany or Hungary, these vessels have either been taken out of service or "cannibalised" to make good shortages of spare parts. This situation has been compounded by the disintegration of the economy and decline in output. Indeed, declining output was responsible for the crisis in the heavy industry and building sectors. In Ukraine, 86 per cent of inland waterway traffic was related to the building sector. Furthermore, the statistics reflect the disruption caused by wars and embargoes. The embargo on river traffic on the Danube, for example, was widely complied with and resulted in the closure of scheduled shipping lines.

Following the break-up of the former Yugoslavia in 1992, some countries such as Serbia have not issued statistics on inland waterway traffic. The collapse in eastern Europe would therefore seem to be linked to the economic and political problems which this region is currently experiencing. Since 1995, traffic levels have gradually started to recover, as confirmed by the statistics for 1996. The decline observed since 1989 would therefore seem to have been a temporary phenomenon and probably a direct result of economic restructuring. Economic growth over the next few years will stimulate traffic levels. As in the case of Poland, whose GDP grew by 7 per cent in 1995, average growth in all these countries should amount to at least 5 per cent a year during the initial stages of the recovery. It should be noted, however, that the per capita GDP of Slovenia, the highest in the area, is still 3.3 times lower than that of France.

Table 5a. **Statistics for worldwide inland waterway traffic in 1992**

Country	Tonnage transported Metric tonne thousands			Tonnage per kilometre T-km millions		
	Total	Push-towed	%	Total	Push-towed	%
Germany (former FRG & GDR)	229 924	63 628	27.7	57 239	8 956	15.6
Austria	6 705	1 862	27.8	1 462	364	24.9
Belgium	89 496	18 153	20.3	5 083	851	16.7
France	70 900	11 196	15.8	8 631	1 611	18.7
Hungary	9 097	*7 324*	*80.5*	1 495	*1 204*	*80.5*
Luxembourg	10 895	1 450	13.3	338	44	13.0
Netherlands	262 201	60 239	23.0	33 570	7 118	21.2
Poland	7 875	6 890	87.5	751	422	56.2
Switzerland	8 694	*3 927*	*45.2*	50	*23*	*45.2*
Czech Republic	5 283	*4 031*	*76.3*	1 790	*1 366*	*76.3*
Slovakia	*1 490*	*1 490*	*100*	*1 188*	*1 188*	*100*
Croatia	501	245	49.0	52	25	49.0
United Kingdom	5 910			200		
Other European countries	9 597			2 792		
Belarus	*1 810*			*990*		
Ukraine	65 728	42 821	65.1	11 981	2 831	23.6
Baltic States	2 272			450		
Other countries of the former USSR	583	583		27	27	
Russia	307 549	213 036	69.3	135 792	48 061	35.4
Total for Europe including Russia	**1 096 510**			**253 881**		
United States	633 093	602 970	95.2	435 940	*409 907*	94.0
Total	**1 745 311**			**699 848**		

Figures in *italics* estimated - NPI/30 June 1996/p. 348 - UN Statistics.

The transport sector in Europe is therefore set to grow rapidly and the inland waterways will have their part to play in this expansion.

1.2. Principal traffic flows

The volume of traffic in the Rhine corridor amounted to 291.7 million tonnes in 1992 and the volume of container traffic (see Figure and Table 5b below) has enjoyed rapid and sustained growth, rising by almost 1 million TEU in 1996.

Figure and Table 5b.
Trend in traffic along the Rhine corridor and worldwide

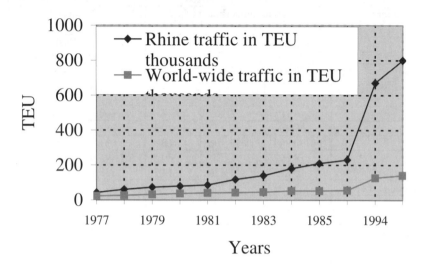

	1977	1978	1979	1980	1981	1982
Traffic on Rhine in TEU thousands	43	60	73	80	86	118
Traffic world-wide in TEU Millions	22.9	26.4	31.9	37.1	40.8	42.8

	1983	1984	1985	1986	1994	1995
Traffic on Rhine in TEU thousands	140	180	210	230	670	800
Traffic world-wide in TEU millions	45.5	52.7	52.7	55.7	127	141

Traffic on the Moselle amounted to 15.4 million tonnes in 1995; in 1996, traffic on the Moselle and the French stretch of the Rhine amounted to 18.6 million tonnes.

The South-East corridor includes the Rhine-Main-Danube corridor as well as the Danube itself.

Traffic on the Rhine-Main-Danube Canal grew by over 22 per cent in 1995, and 6 278 000 tonnes of freight passed through the Viereth Lock.

Traffic on the Danube in 1993 amounted to 23.8 million tonnes, a steep decline that reflected the impact on the embargo (69.6 million tonnes in 1990). This situation has now been reversed. Traffic levels have recovered on the German stretch of the Danube and in 1995 amounted to 6.5 million tonnes, a 20 per cent increase on 1992. Freight tonnages at the international level grew by 32 per cent.

The volume of traffic on the Austrian Danube amounted to 7.7 million tonnes in 1994. The port of Vienna handled 6 million tonnes of freight, the port of Linz 4.2 million tonnes and Krems 0.37 million tonnes. Traffic in 1995 amounted to 8.7 million tonnes, almost up to the record level of 1989 (9.1 million tonnes) -- despite the crisis in Yugoslavia. Austria benefited from its accession to the European Union by becoming a major platform for the redistribution of flows to the Visegrad countries. Traffic to and from South-East Europe is also starting to recover. In 1995, the container traffic between Austria and the Benelux ports handled by Wasserkombi alone amounted to 12 000 TEU, an increase of 33 per cent compared with the 9 000 TEU carried by Wasserkombi in 1993. This rapid growth may be held back, however, by lack of adequate clearance beneath three railway bridges. Traffic on the Hungarian Danube amounted to almost 11 million tonnes a year, 3 million tonnes of which were loaded and unloaded in Hungarian ports. Traffic on the Tisza is steadily declining.

Along the East-West corridor, the *Mittellandkanal* traffic amounted to 9 million tonnes. This corridor is connected to the Elbe, on which the volume of traffic has tripled. In 1995, traffic on the Elbe amounted to 10.238 million tonnes, of which 1.9 million tonnes upstream of Hamburg and 8.3 million tonnes downstream. 3.3 million tonnes were transported on the Elbe itself and 4.9 million tonnes on the lateral canal. The breakdown of this flow included 0.7 million tonnes to Slovakia and 0.6 million tonnes to the new *Länder* and Berlin. Depending on the waterway, annual traffic grew at a rate of 15-20 per cent.

The volume of traffic on the North-South corridor (Rotterdam/Antwerp/France) rose substantially. In 1996, 750 000 TEU were transported through the Great Delta. This corridor has now virtually reached saturation point and additional capacity will need to be provided. Overall traffic amounted to 60 million tonnes.

Traffic grew substantially on some of the more isolated waterways, such as the Albert Canal, which carried 33 million tonnes in 1994, whereas the level on others, and on the Seine and Rhône waterways, remained modest because of their lack of interconnections to other waterways.

1.3. Markets

1.3.1   The least successful markets

Oil and gas

The oil and gas transport market within the European Union is declining. The sale of NATO's pipelines led to a crisis in the tanker fleet. Tanker traffic along the Danube, on the other hand, is staging a recovery and the energy requirements of the eastern European countries will continue to rise for many years to come.

Building and construction materials

The trend in such traffic in western Europe contrasts sharply with that in the eastern and central European countries, where major urban and infrastructure renewal projects are now starting up. Although the volume of traffic in this sector remains high in western Europe, the rate of growth is starting to level off. The building and construction sector is susceptible to changes in the economic climate. In the major towns and cities on the inland waterway network in France, almost 90 per cent of sand and gravel supplies are carried by water. While it seems unlikely that there will be any scope for the inland waterways to increase their market share in western European countries, it is possible that, depending upon the rate of economic growth, they may gain market share in the CEECs, even if that share is currently still modest. Such markets may well be limited to the local level.

In France, the volume of sand and gravel transported along the North-South corridor (Nord/Pas de Calais/Picardy/Paris region) is growing as a result of the depletion of local deposits and the provisions of French environmental legislation (Water Act).

The ore transport sector is declining in response to changes in the economy and the market has been shrinking since 1994 with the conversion of European sites to electric-arc steelmaking processes, in which scrap iron is used rather than mineral ore.

Potential demand remains high, however, particularly from iron and steel mills in the Liège region, the Saar or the Ruhr, Lorraine and the Danube countries. Ore is essential for the production of flat products used by the car, packing, white goods and pipeline industries. Furthermore, European steelmakers are specialised in the production of specialty steels. This type of traffic may therefore offer scope for growth.

1.3.2   Markets now recovering after a period of stagnation

Coal demand from electricity utilities and the steel industry now seems to be starting to recover. Reduced coal production in Germany, the gradual phasing-out of subsidies to the mining industry and the abolition of the *Huttenvertag* (the mandatory requirement that German steelmakers buy their coal from the Ruhr) should lead to a massive increase in imports of much cheaper coal from abroad. However, EMO, which seems to have forgotten that it made its name in "just-in-time" services for both containerised transport and ore transport (e.g. Cockerill Sambre), has recently invested in rail facilities in Rotterdam and it would therefore seem that the inland waterways can expect to face competition from the railways in this market. NS Cargo is attempting to capitalise on the disadvantages for inland water transport of fluctuations in water levels and periods when waterways are ice-bound; from an environmental standpoint, however, the inland waterways have the edge over rail. The LASH (Lighter Aboard SHip) system might be one way in which to increase supply in the inland waterway network, or vessel-to-vessel transhipment, a technique that is used all too infrequently.

1.3.3   Promising markets

Promising markets exist in many sectors:

- The agro-food sector is a growth market, as shown by rising volumes of traffic along the North Sea-Black Sea corridor and the transport of soya between Rotterdam and Hungary. The agro-food terminal in Budapest, set up by the privatised Hungarian distributor, Masped, is now a hub for the distribution of agricultural and agro-food produce in Europe. Masped works in collaboration with the Hungarian charterer for navigation on the Danube, Mahart. The share of the agro-food products in transport flows is rising, particularly in terms of export flows. Cereal flows, despite the Uruguay Round agreements, seem to be rising again. Since 1996, trade flows between the CEECs and the NIS and Russia appear to have recovered. Cereal production in this area is now higher than the 1989 level. Yields are also rising rapidly. In Poland, for example, they have risen from 30 cwt in 1992 to 36 cwt in 1996. This trend looks set to continue. It is worth bearing in mind that before 1914 this area was a major exporter of cereals;

- Emergence of new oil and gas transport flows between Rotterdam and Belgrade;
- The transportation of cement between the ports of South-East Europe and the ports on the Danube and also from western Europe is growing;
- Dangerous goods: recent accidents have accelerated the trend towards the use of inland waterways for such consignments;
- Chemicals: there have been gains in market share in all countries, particularly the Netherlands, at the expense of road, and this trend may continue. French carriers are unanimous in claiming that, given the size and power of the European chemicals industry, the potential market is enormous;
- Iron and steel products: Austria is a major source of flows of iron and steel products and completion of the restructuring of the iron and steel industry in the countries along the Danube is fuelling growth in the market. European manufacturers are increasingly moving towards the top end of the market, i.e. specialty steels. French carriers are experimenting with the use of containers in this sector. The LASH system has recently been introduced for export flows between ports in North-West Europe, notably Dunkirk, and the CEECs;
- The transport of wastes is now a growing market following the introduction of recent EU legislation on waste disposal;
- There is strong growth along all corridors, including those in the CEECs, in the containerised transport of a wide variety of goods. In some cases, the traffic consists in the transport of products to central and eastern Europe which cross the same border at least twice, first as semi-finished, then as finished products and perhaps a third time as packaged goods. Even in France, the volume of such traffic, measured in TEU, grew by 24 per cent in 1996;
- RoRo traffic on the Rhine is increasing, while that on the Danube has resumed with the reinstatement of scheduled trailer transport services on the Danube between Vidin and the ports of Linz and Passau. Such services are even scheduled to be introduced in France along the Rhône. There has also been a recovery and strong growth in combined transport services to Regensburg, where infrastructural modernisation is now nearing completion.

The rapid and strong growth in car manufacturing along this corridor, together with the siting of facilities there by western European and Asian firms, may fuel export flows both eastwards and westwards.

1.3.4 Potential markets or goods now suitable for transport by inland waterway

The markets are primarily situated in maritime ports, although there are also important niche markets in distribution.

- Combined river and ocean-going barge services: these services are aimed at transport flows within Europe, around the Mediterranean basin and to the northern seaboard of Morocco. They allow goods to be transported, without transhipment, from firm to firm as full cargoes by either weight or volume. Moreover, such traffic flows are highly competitive, except in one or two cases due to the existence on certain routes (e.g. the Seine) of unjustified taxes which should be abolished. River and maritime barge traffic is not limited solely to cereals, scrap metal, pulp or timber;
- The transport of containerised goods is increasingly becoming a feature of traffic on the inland waterways. Although currently modest, this type of traffic offers considerable scope for growth and could concern many types of North-South as well as East-West flows. Most goods can be transported by container, given the extremely wide range of containers now available;
- There is much ground to be made up in the transport of consumer goods, despite the numerous examples of the transportation of such goods in Germany. The best known example is that of Neckerman. In France, La Redoute and Auchan have recently begun to make use of this mode. Any type of product within this category of goods can be transported by river;
- Food and flour products (pre-slung flour) could generate considerable traffic flows;
- Dangerous goods (ash, slag, nuclear wastes and fuels, etc.) should preferably be routed by inland waterway;
- Another market lies in the transport of cement;
- Combined river or river/sea transport offers a viable alternative to road transport.

1.4. Transport supply -- Fleets

Fleets in western Europe are currently declining, or have already all declined in size in order to adjust to the new structure of traffic flows in which the share of bulk goods is tending to fall. In contrast, fleets are having to adapt to higher demand for the transport of manufactured goods, usually containerised. This trend has required the restructuring of fleets. A shake-down of the EU fleet is a prerequisite for market liberalisation. After some delay, the EU partly took over the initiative from governments and introduced a scrapping scheme: Directive No. 1101/89, the "Scrap and build" Ruling 1102/89, Ruling 3690/92, Ruling 2254/96 (1996, 1997 and 1998 restructuring plan), Ruling 241/97 of 10 February 1997.

This restructuring is now almost completed on the Rhine, the Rhône (Tables 6 and 7) and in the Netherlands, where the waterway sector is experiencing renewed growth. The number of inland waterway operators is increasing in the Netherlands, where it has risen from 4 484 to 4 575. The most remarkable development in the Netherlands has been the increase in the private barge fleet, where the number of family-operated vessels has risen from 4 026 to 4 100. In the two to maximum ten vessels category, the number of operators has risen from 428 to 450. The size of the overall fleet, however, is down slightly. The number of self-propelled barges has fallen from 4 665 to 4 600 and the number of push-towed barges from 741 to 700; in contrast, the number of towed barges has risen from 386 to 400. This is not yet the case in Germany, where wholesale restructuring is still in progress.

The western European fleet is equipping itself with the new generation of self-propelled push-tow barges that are better adapted to the needs of containerised transport. They are better suited to carriers' requirements, notably for just-in-time deliveries. On Class III waterways, the modular self-propelled, self-unloading barge designed for this type of traffic looks set to be a great success. Push-tow barges are primarily used for shipments of bulk goods. The average size of vessels is increasing in order to improve their competitiveness, but this increase is not systematically aimed at the largest category of vessel.

The East European fleets need to be modernised. Barges are often towed and technical standards, particularly safety regulations, are still inadequate. In some countries, such as Poland, the size of vessels is relatively small. Average tonnages on the Danube are much higher. Almost all fleets have been privatised. The type of problem encountered varies from one network to another.

In both eastern and western Europe, carriers or private operators are seeking to improve their competitiveness.

Table 6. **Fleet composition**

Country	Number of units		Gross carrying capacity (million metric tonnes)			Average size of a river barge unit (tonnes)
	Total	Push-towed	Total	Push-towed	%	
Germany (former GDR & GFR)	3 749	1 418	3 328.7	1 136.4	34.1	888
Austria	225	140	250.2	206.4	82.5	1 112
Belgium	1 845	292	1 475	374.6	25.4	799
France	2 878	989	1551.7	692.1	44.6	539
Hungary	249	145	251.2	*202.2*	*80.5*	1 009
Luxembourg	28	0	28.6	0	0	1 021
Netherlands	6 534	1 109	5 818.1	1 525	26.2	890
Poland	2 102	1 069	812.4	340.5	41.9	386
Switzerland	156	69	281.4	127.1	45.2	1 804
Czech Republic	*543*	*469*	*321.6*	*245.4*	*76.3*	*592*
Slovakia	309	*309*	376.2	*376.2*	*100*	1 217
Croatia	189	107	83.1	40.7	49	440
United Kingdom	830		205			247
Other European countries	274		370.6			1 356
Belarus						
Ukraine	765	347	762	372.7	48.9	996
Baltic States	107	51	1.4	0.6	42.9	13
Russia	24 559	2 647				
Other countries of the former USSR	115	114	30.9	30.8	99.7	269
United States	34 387	28 615	42 111	40 190	95.4	1 225

Figures in *italics* estimated.

Table 7. **Rhine fleet (in tonnes)**

Country	Self-propelled			Barges			Total		
	1980	1996	%	1980	1996	%	1980	1996	%
Netherlands	2 800 705	4 110 904	+46.8	495 206	863 612	+74.4	3 295 911	4 974 516	+50.9
Germany	2 603 321	2 078 559	-20.2	304 362	511 364	+68.0	2 907 683	2 589 923	-10.9
Belgium	1 228 353	1 249 822	+1.7	128 436	177 623	+38.3	1 356 789	1 427 445	+5.2
France	286 625	272 431	-5.9	98 509	59 422	-39.7	388 134	331 853	-14.5
Switzerland	404 447	176 564	-56.3	93 867	10 770	-88.5	498 314	187 334	-62.4
Total	7 326 451	7 888 280	+7.7	1 120 380	1 622 791	+44.8	8 446 831	9 511 071	+12.6

Source: NPI/30 Sep 1996/page 501.

Table 8. **Trend in the average size of vessels in the Rhine fleet between 1980 and 1996**

	Self-propelled		Variation		Barges		Variation		All vessels		Variation	
	1980	1996	T	%	1980	1996	t	%	1980	1996	t	%
	t	t			t	t			t	t		
Netherlands	623	942	+319	+51.2	1 281	2 303	+1 022	+79.8	719	1 142	+423	+58.8
Germany	939	1 127	+188	+20.0	1 850	879	-971	-52.5	1 035	1 031	-4	-0.4
Belgium	725	833	+108	+14.9	2 039	2 631	+592	+29.0	772	982	+210	+27.2
France	396	437	+41	+10.4	2 074	1 857	-217	-10.5	589	570	-19	-3.2
Switzerland	1 366	1 940	+574	+42.0	1 916	1 958	+42	+2.2	1 503	1 942	+439	+29.2

Table 9. Fleet capacity of selected countries with a fully operational inland waterway network

	Austria	Belgium	France	Germany	Netherlands	Switzerland
1975	208 850	2 321 000	2 940 000	4 221 812	5 117 000	575 000
1980	195 790	1 844 000	2 537 052	3 671 963	4 900 000	592 000
1985	237 711	1 729 412	2 308 044	3 276 622	5 447 000	579 685
1990	257 924	1 523 301	1 652 600	3 055 923	6 113 000	321 508
1991	251 414	1 465 099	1 535 420	2 955 517	5 994 000	290 341
1992					5 840 000	281 719
1993					5 842 000	

Table 10. Number of vessels in selected countries with a fully operational inland waterway network

	Austria	Belgium	France	Germany	Netherlands	Switzerland
1975	203	4 182	6 563	4 786	8 146	423
1980	194	3 001	5 224	3 812	6 535	394
1985	213	2 513	4 729	3 143	6 371	335
1990	210	1 778	3 068	2 723	6 282	169
1991	204	1 639	2 813	2 574	6 011	151
1992					5 681	144
1993					5 524	

Table 11. **Trend in the average capacity of vessels**

	Austria	Belgium	France	Germany	Netherlands	Switzerland
1975	1 029	555	447	882	628	1 359
1980	1 009	615	486	963	750	1 503
1985	1 116	688	488	1 043	855	1 730
1990	1 228	857	539	1 122	973	1 902
1991	1 232	894	546	1 148	997	1 923
1992					1 028	1 956

2. FACTORS LIABLE TO SLOW THE GROWTH OF INLAND WATERWAYS

Physical geography, the distinctive characteristics of transport by inland waterway, the structure of the industry, fleet composition, the attitudes of charterers, the restructuring in progress in the CEECs, the transport policy of the EU and EU Member States can all conspire to hold back the development of transport by inland waterway.

2.1. The constraints of physical geography

– The topography and uneven density of the hydrographic system can preclude the use of this mode of transport in certain areas;
– The unpredictability of weather conditions and water supply: floods, such as those which occurred in January and February 1995, and the freezing conditions that prevailed during the winter of 1994-1995, brought the entire European fleet practically to a standstill.

Problems arising from the depth of river channels still remain. On the German stretch of the Danube between Straubing and Vilshofen, a draught of 2.50 m can only be accommodated for 45 days a year. A similar problem is faced in Hungary and on the river Elbe. Navigation on the Rhine is sometimes disrupted by periods of very low water.

2.2. Distinctive characteristics of the mode

The legendary slowness of inland waterway navigation, encourages the belief that it is unsuitable for just-in-time deliveries to firms.

2.3. A highly fragmented industry and fleet

The structure of the inland water transport industry in western Europe is far too fragmented. French and Belgian operators need to support the co-operatives now starting to emerge in the industry, on similar lines to those already in place in the Netherlands and Germany, in order to derive maximum benefit from the latest logistical tools, to operate as lines and to provide efficient services. They need to embrace the liberal aspects of the market and, accordingly, must abandon the system of chartering by rotation. The transport market in France was opened up to the market place under the Act of 12 July 1994 and the first Decree of 30 September 1996. *Voies Navigables de France* is helping operators to adapt to the opening-up of the market.

In eastern European countries, the liberalisation of the market calls for the creation of dynamic chartering systems. On the Danube, alliances with shipowners from the Rhine appear to be promoting such a development. The rules which countries such as Romania apply to foreign fleets need to be abolished. In addition, greater efforts must be made to take account of the existence of inland water transport, since, for a variety of reasons, many of the current transport support programmes provide little assistance to this mode. The EU, and also the BERD and BIRD must gain a greater awareness of the potential contribution that inland waterways can make to protection of the environment.

The current market framework, whatever it might be, must be dismantled, although safeguards will need to be put in place. Chartering by rotation and all other restrictions must be abolished in favour of freedom of contract (Directive 96/75/CE).

2.4. Socioeconomic constraints

The gradual loss of interest in this mode on the part of charterers has benefited road transport. France is an example of this trend. Marketing campaigns are needed to draw people's attention to the fact that the inland waterways are a multimodal and modern mode of transport. Many Belgian charterers have stopped using inland water transport because of the complexity of the tariff systems and the constraints of the chartering by rotation system.

In central and eastern European Countries (CEECs), transport operators and charterers are increasingly turning to road transport. The shipping companies, which were tightly regulated by government under the former political system, have found it hard to adapt to the new market conditions. They have been unable to respond to demand, a situation which has been exacerbated by the obsolete facilities available in ports. In addition, their reconversion has been held back by the embargo on traffic on the Danube. Only the most dynamic companies have been able to restructure their operations, in some cases through agreements with western operators. The volume of freight transported by rail in 1994 declined by a massive 55 per cent in 1994 compared with 1989 for much the same reasons, although in this particular case the situation was compounded by the rail sector's lack of interoperability. Road transport declined by merely 20 per cent and its conversion has been helped by low fuel prices. State-owned groups in the haulage sector offer tariffs at less than cost price and a large number of small firms have been set up as very little capital is needed to create new businesses. Road transport is reaping the benefits of the economic recovery now starting to take shape and has gained a dominant position that it is unlikely to relinquish for the foreseeable future. The Crete Conference on Pan-European Networks, held in March 1994, appears to have given priority, firstly, to road corridors and, secondly, to rail corridors. The inland waterways would seem to be the poor relations.

The inland waterway industry offers little scope for job creation. To transport a million tonne/km requires twenty people in the road sector, two in the rail sector and 0.5 in the inland waterway sector.

As a mode of transport, the inland waterways have little political influence, except in countries where priority is given to the environment and where traffic flows are so enormous that inland waterways are an essential component of the transport sector.

2.5. Attitude of maritime port authorities towards inland waterways

Port authorities may sometimes have a negative attitude towards inland waterways and may be unwilling to invest in certain types of infrastructure, as may be seen by the reluctance of the port of Le Havre and a number of German ports to proceed with the construction of infrastructure. The port of Le Havre is opposed to construction of the Seine-North Canal out of a fear of increased competition from Antwerp and Rotterdam, a longstanding problem which has prevented the French and Belgian networks from achieving interoperability for over a century but which, in the process, has failed to prevent traffic from being diverted elsewhere. The potential diversion of traffic away from Hamburg and Bremen explains Germany's opposition to the construction of a direct link between Rotterdam and the *Mittellandkanal* via the *Twentekanaal*.

Among the opposing factors are the high costs of transhipment in certain maritime ports, where the hiring of dockers under the same regime applicable to ocean-going vessels imposes handling costs three times higher than those in inland river ports and higher than those applicable per lorry- or wagon-load. In view of this, the use of maritime cargo hoists must be priced at marginal cost. In addition, there is the cumulative time lost in waiting for vessels to be loaded or unloaded in ports with several terminals as a result of priority being given to the use of cargo hoists for ocean-going vessels, including small vessels used for cabotage with a carrying capacity of 50 TEU, whereas river vessels can carry up to 350 TEU. It is also often impossible to carry out direct transhipment. The lack or extreme scarcity of appropriate river terminals is to be deplored. Crossing through ports poses problems, notably in Antwerp where the tax on push-towing (FB 100) is too high.

There is also considerable ground to make up in the development of river-maritime traffic and there are very substantial price distortions per tonne transported between different river corridors. Transportation on the Seine costs three times as much as that on the Rhine (FF 15.5/t compared with FF 5.4/t on the Rhine).

2.6. Delays in developing EU transport policy

EU policy only really started to develop from 1985 onwards. This delay is probably attributable to the desire of Member States to pursue their own approaches.

The individualistic policies adopted by countries led to priority being given to certain modes. In France, inland waterways were sacrificed, as was maritime shipping. This helped to keep in place a highly bureaucratic system of commercial legislation and to perpetuate restrictive conditions of market access. The fact that this mode was highly versatile was not taken into account in the amortisation of investments (see Figure 1 below).

At present while, admittedly, a European infrastructural plan has been published, implementing this plan remains something of a utopian ideal since no provision has been made for financing mechanisms. The long overdue European transport policy, particularly with regard to inland waterway transport, is characterised by a lack of harmonization between the policy of individual Member States towards inland waterways. Following the total liberalisation of coastal trade, there is no longer any justification for the application of differing legal and commercial regimes (1 January 1995). The lack of a multilateral agreement with CEECs is also paralysing growth in traffic.

Figure 1. **Versatility of inland waterways**

TRANSPORTS	Blends perfectly into landscape
	Improves road traffic conditions
PROTECTION OF THE ENVIRONMENT	Alternative to road traffic initial aim of diverting 15to20% of road traffic
	Less air and noise pollution
	Hydropower

EXTRAORDINARY VERSATILITY OF INLAND WATERWAYS

DEVELOPMENT OF THE ENVIRONMENT
- Protection against spates and floods
- Improvement of living environment
- Development of valleys and natural heritage
- Town planning and waterfront developm.in towns
- Support for low water

ECONOMIC ROLES
- Provision of sites for industrial parks and logistical centres
- Tourism, pleasure boats

Water supply
- to towns
- to industry
- to agriculture irrigation
- for recreational purposes/fishing

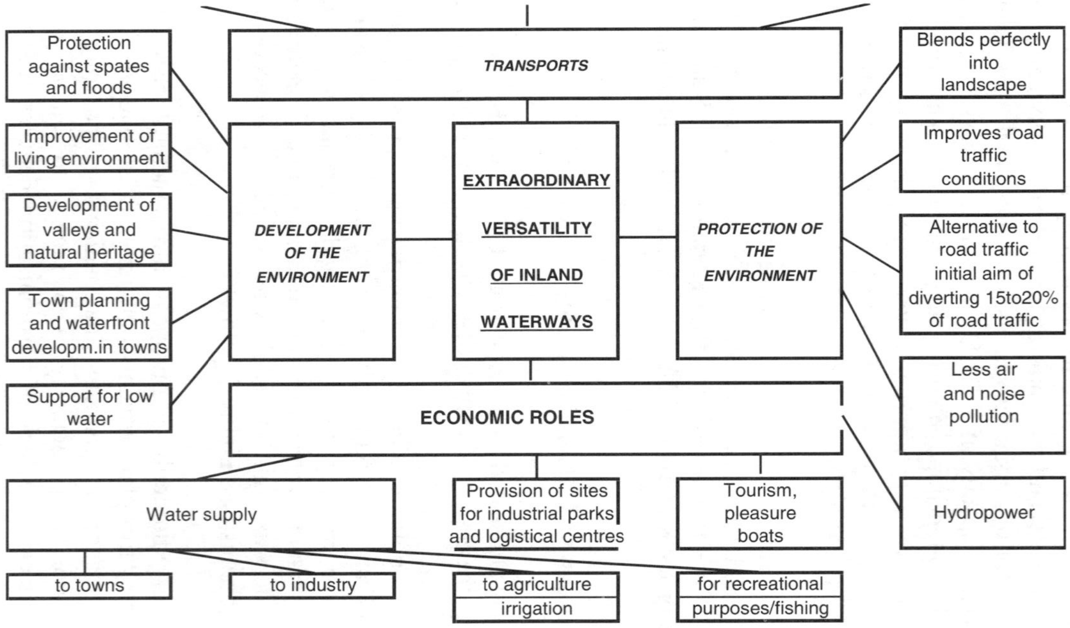

This leads to price distortions that are damaging for both river traffic and river-maritime transport. It is also a problem keenly felt in certain East European countries which have adopted an individualistic approach.

2.7. Lack of harmonization between the commissions supervising international rivers

One particular example of this is the lack of harmonization between the Commission for the Navigation of the Rhine and the Danube Commission. The harmonization of rules within the greater European Area, with a view to stimulating river transport, should only be based on widespread adoption of the Mannheim Convention, after negotiation between the different partners. At present, the stand-off between the European Union and the oldest intergovernmental body, the CCR, is particularly unfortunate.

2.8. Lack of interoperability and outmoded nature of some networks

The delays that France, Italy, and the countries of central and eastern Europe have allowed to build up with regard to the modernisation of their infrastructure and development of efficient corridors remain substantial. For the time being, the planned modernisation of national networks is still at the proposal stage. The indefinite postponement of the Polish programme is a worrying development. The Czech Republic has embarked upon major restructuring of the industry and there are now some forty private operators. By the year 2000, Hungary hopes to modernise its inland waterway network, its ports and its fleet and to increase navigable water depths on the Danube to 2.5 m. Regulating the Danube must be a priority.

In France, the lack of a network of wide-gauge canals and the existence of four isolated networks with no interconnections, other than by river or by sea, have had a major adverse effect on traffic densities.

Consequently, France, with 1 707 km of wide-gauge waterways, has the shortest network of such waterways of all the countries of North-West Europe and is the country which makes least use of its waterways. Over two-thirds of the networks of Germany and the Netherlands consist of Class VI, V and IV waterways. Lacking major river corridors, French maritime ports have local hinterlands and face competition in their own regions from the ports in the Rhine Delta (Rotterdam, Antwerp and Zeebrugge), which enjoy a concentration of transport flows for all maritime and surface modes. The latter generate activity in forelands and hinterlands where the concept of distance is viewed in

107

terms of cost rather than space and time. The secondary effect of this is to divert large flows of traffic away from France, which is unable to attract the transit flows that can act as a catalyst for development.

Table 12. **Non-interconnected river barge network in France accessible to convoys of 3 000 tonnes and above**

	Length in km	Traffic density (1 000 t/km)
Main networks		
Seine river basin	558*	5 088
North	214	7 523
Moselle and Rhine	338	20 045
Saône and Rhône	402	641
Secondary networks		
Loire Estuary	56	6.6
Gironde, Dordogne and Garonne	85	52.7
Total	1 707	

* Including the Seine Estuary.
Source: VNF, 1995.

Of these networks, only the Rhine network (Class VI) enjoys good interconnections with other areas in Europe. As a result, traffic densities in the Rhine network are 31 times higher than those in an isolated Class VI waterway such as the Saône-Rhône corridor. The Rhine and Moselle network would have even higher densities if it were connected to the other networks in France (see Table 13).

Lack of sufficient water depth also acts as a brake on the competitiveness of the network. The same comment applies to the Dunkirk Canal in Valenciennes. These shortcomings totally cancel out the potential profitability of the investments made.

Table 13. **Multiplying factor for the impact of**
interconnections on traffic densities*

	Coefficient x traffic density
Interconnection of a Class VI waterway in a Class VI network with a Class I waterway	31.00
Interconnection of a Class VI waterway with two networks (one Class IV the other Class I)	11.74
Interconnection of a Class VI waterway with a network by means of a Class I waterway	7.94

*   Factor defined by relating the density of traffic on a Class VI corridor to a corridor
       of the same class that is more or less isolated -- a weighting coefficient allows
       account to be taken of the varying degrees of interconnection.

2.9. Fierce competition from rail and road

Instead of encouraging competition, the aim should be to work towards
making modes complement each other.

3. WHAT ASSETS DO INLAND WATERWAYS HAVE
THAT MIGHT STIMULATE THE MARKET?

3.1. A mode of transport that can help safeguard the environment

3.1.1   Waterway transport generates the lowest external costs of all
transport modes, even though at first sight the infrastructure costs might seem
enormous. This finding is borne out by detailed studies[1] of the environmental
impact of different modes of transport which the Rhine countries, particularly
Germany and Switzerland, have been carrying out for more than a decade.

These studies illustrate, firstly, the costs[2] that are not covered by specific
income in different modes of inland transport in 1985, at a time when they were
lower than at present and, secondly, emissions of gases such as CO_2 in different
surface and air transport modes.

The results show (Table 14) that, in Germany, subsidies worth
DM 5 billion, i.e. FF 17 billion, were provided for expenditure on infrastructure
for the surface transport of goods: DM 1.5 billion for road, covering 82 per cent

of infrastructure costs; DM 2.6 billion for rail, covering merely 40 per cent of the infrastructure costs; and DM 0.9 billion for inland waterways, which covered no more than 10 per cent of the costs. Translated into t-km, the subsidies amounted to 1.1 Pf per t-km for road, 1.8 Pf per t-km for inland waterways and 4.1 Pf per t-km for rail.

Table 14. **Coverage of infrastructure costs for goods transport in 1985**

DM millions	Rail	Road	Inland waterways	All modes
Income from Infrastructure	1 765	6 894	104	8 763
Expenditure on Infrastructure	4 409	8 383	975	13 763
Coverage	40%	82.2%	10.7%	63.7%
Traffic in million T/km	64.5	132.2	48.2	244.9
In Pf per t/km				
Income	2.7	5.2	0.2	3.6
Expenditure	6.8	6.3	2.0	5.6
Expenditure not Covered	4.1	1.1	1.8	2.0

However, the situation is reversed in terms of external costs (Table 15). The road sector is very poorly placed in Germany. At DM 6.5 billion a year, it is the surface mode which generates by far the highest level of nuisances for the community and which makes no specific allocation either to reduce these nuisances or to compensate users. Translated into t/km, the highest costs are those of the road sector. If inland waterways are taken as base 1, then rail is at 4.2 and road at 18.9.

These findings demonstrate the urgency with which unused inland waterway capacity must be mobilised and the need to develop such infrastructure in order to improve the quality of the environment. The internalisation of costs can ensure an excellent rate of return on waterway infrastructure.

Table 15. **External social costs of goods traffic in**

Total costs	DM millions			Costs in t-km		
	Rail	**Road**	**Waterway**	**Rail**	**Road**	
Accidents	75	2 500	7	0.160	1.89	
Noise	411	489		0.637	0.37	
Air pollution	114	1 923	102	0.177	1.45	0.212
Soil pollution	566		0.428			
Severance effects	81		0.061			
Land use	14	84	0.022	0.064		
Total	614	5 643	109	0.952	4.629	0.226

3.1.2   Air pollution

CO_2 emissions in the inland waterway sector are equivalent to those in the rail sector. These levels are overestimated, however, since German electricity is mainly generated in fossil-fired power plants. In terms of t/km, rail and inland waterways emit five times less CO_2 and CH_4 than road and 28 times less than the air transport sector. In absolute terms, CO_2 emissions in Germany attributable to freight transport in 1985 amounted to 30 million tonnes for road, 2.4 million tonnes for rail and 2.1 million tonnes for inland waterways.

In the inland waterway sector, however, such pollution could be reduced by using electricity to power boats. Batteries could serve as ballast and their weight, which is penalising for a lorry, poses no problems in this mode of transport. The time needed to load and unload goods is enough to cover the recharging time for conventional lead batteries.

3.1.3   Noise pollution

Waterways are of major interest with regard to noise pollution in that a push-towed convoy of barges, for the time that it is in motion, is capable of transporting 4 400 tonnes of freight, i.e. the equivalent of 220 twenty-tonne trucks, without generating any noise. This advantage alone justifies use of the mode.

A study comparing the noise generated by a convoy of river barges transporting 4 400 tonnes of goods at a commercial speed of 9 km/h with that generated by a fleet of 158 articulated lorries travelling at 90 km/h at 35-minute intervals was used to plot an intensity/duration curve for the noise to which a person located 50 m from the road would be subjected. With road transport, the

productivity increases through advanced shipbuilding techniques and new technologies facilitating land/sea and land/river interfaces and *vice versa*. Use of the inland waterways lends added significance to the idea of up-river ports.

3.2.3   *Inland waterways are a competitive mode of transport*

Inland waterways can readily internalise external costs.

3.2.4   *Inland waterways are not a slow mode of transport*

Two or three extra days are sufficient for supplementary pre- or post-carriage, a short period of time compared with the 21 days for the maritime leg between Singapore and Le Havre or Rotterdam.

Navigation can proceed seven days a week, which makes inland waterways as fast a mode of transport as road haulage, which is obliged to cease transport operations every Sunday. An example of this is the service provided by Logiseine which leaves Le Havre on Saturday night and arrives in Gennevilliers on Monday morning.

3.2.5   *Safety*

Inland waterways are the safest mode of transport, particularly for the transportation of chemicals and dangerous goods.

3.2.6   *Surplus capacity*

The inland waterways have surplus capacity.

3.2.7   *Integration*

The inland waterways can be perfectly integrated into the modern logistical chains operated by the major charterers, as may be shown by the inventory of containers carried on river barges: beverages, household appliances, computers, video equipment, clothing, a wide variety of manufactured goods, frozen foods, chilled products.

The use of IT systems enables goods shipments to be accurately tracked, increases navigational safety and productivity, while at the same time allowing supply to be better matched to demand through clearing houses.

3.2.8   Concentration of flows

The concentration of flows, which has fuelled growth in conventional modes of transport, can also work to the advantage of the inland waterways. Container barges on the Rhine have an average carrying capacity of 160 TEU, equivalent to around three container trains or a two-kilometre convoy of lorries. Such barges could therefore meet the needs of maritime shippers; a 6 000-TEU container ship is equivalent to a 200 km convoy of lorries if safety regulations are properly respected. As a result, the inland waterways are an ideal partner for Main Ports and mega-carriers. Convoys of 380-TEU can now be seen on the Rhine.

3.2.9   Flexibility

The modular nature of convoys is such that inland waterways offer great flexibility in terms of the routing and frequency of deliveries. Transport operations can easily be modified. In France, for example, CNC-Transports is apparently seeking to capitalise on synergies with river waterway operators of container vessels with regard to shipments to and from maritime ports. To do this, the company has acquired a 25 per cent stake in Paris Terminal S.A. and a 5 per cent stake in Lyon-Terminal S.A. It hopes to trim excess capacity and to work towards the development of up-river ports.

3.2.10   Multimodal platforms

Inland ports are becoming multimodal platforms managed by logistical operators. Modular self-propelled vessels, fitted with cargo hoists for loading and unloading goods, together with roller barges, dispense with the need for inland ports to be equipped with heavy infrastructure and thus afford greater flexibility.

3.2.11   Territorial development at the European level

Inland waterways can serve as an instrument for development of the European Area from the Atlantic to the Urals at local, regional and national level and also at the level of the current European Union and the future enlarged Union.

At the local level, all the major European metropolitan centres -- such as London, Brussels, Amsterdam, Frankfurt, Berlin, Paris, and tomorrow those of the countries of central and eastern Europe -- are building their urban renewal programmes around their rivers or canal networks. An ever-growing number of cities are attempting to renew links with their waterways or ports. The waterways are the perfect means of removing the demolition rubble generated by urban renewal programmes, provided that shippers and port authorities are

115

prepared to provide logistical support in order to realise the full potential of the waterways as an alternative mode of transport. As suppliers to shippers or port authorities, and perhaps in future for urban mobility, the waterways are one of the keys to solving problems relating to pollution.

3.3. The actors in the modernisation process

The actors in the process of modernisation have a determining role to play: river transport operators, maritime shippers, inland ports, maritime ports, carriers, governments and international organisations.

3.3.1   River transport operators

River transport operators offer services throughout the logistics chain in order and can deliver goods to destination in association with other modes. Inland waterways therefore fit perfectly into combined transport operations. Co-operation with other modes is steadily growing. By way of an example, the European Intermodal Association, a combined transport lobbying organisation, has recently opened itself up to river and maritime shipping.

Operators know how to promote just-in-place and just-in-time deliveries by mobilising all the partners involved.

With regard to container traffic, they began by developing a perfect logistical chain along the Rhine which confounded all initial forecasts.

The first service by an ocean-going container vessel, the US Lines "American Ranger", to Antwerp and to Rotterdam in March 1966 generated interest on all sides and much scepticism. In 1967, transport forecasters estimated that merely 5 per cent of this traffic could be carried by waterway. By 1986, the same organisations were forecasting that the share of river-borne trade in this sector for the Port of Rotterdam would rise from 15 per cent in 1985 to 24 per cent by the year 2000. By 1993, however, this share had already risen above 35 per cent.

This spectacular growth (see Figure and Table 5b), higher than that in ocean-going containerised traffic, can be attributed to the inherent advantages of waterway transport and, above all, to the dynamic approach adopted by shippers and owner-skippers on the Rhine. By as early as the mid-1970s, operators were able to offer customers large, simple-design vessels (Europe I and Europe II type barges) capable of carrying 72 or 90 TEU. This meant that container transport was no longer the exclusive preserve of the road sector. Following the successful launch of these services, the energy crisis and the quality of the services provided helped to fuel growth in this sector and scheduled services were first introduced in 1976-1977.

The development of new technology towards the early 1980s led to the construction of self-propelled tow-push barges, allowing greater flexibility in providing services to more than one terminal in the same port. Convoy-carrying capacity on the Rhine rose to 8 000 tonnes and 288 TEU.

Advances in shipbuilding techniques have led to spectacular gains in productivity: over the past fifteen years there have been three new generations of increasingly sophisticated vessels which have allowed the fleet to match the increase in the size of maritime container ships. Carrying capacity is still continuing to rise and convoys of 380 TEU are now becoming common.

At the same time in the mid-1980s, the major Rhine shippers and owner-operators began to set up groups which, in the face of growing competition, would be able to offer better services. This led to the creation in 1986 of the *Fahrgemeinschaft*, or Rhine Navigation Community, in which the acquisition of freight remained the responsibility of each partner who, in offering a full door-to-door service, was referred to an operator. These operators set up a comprehensive network of terminals.

However, this success is also attributable to close collaboration between maritime shippers.

Table 16. **Rhine river shippers providing scheduled services to or from Antwerp**

Carrier	Represented in Antwerp by	Number of vessels and capacity in TEU	Number of departures per week	Sailings	Destinations
Fahrgemeinschaft Niederrhein CCS Rhinecontainer Häger und Schmidt Haniel	Rhenus Belgium Neptune Shipping RKE De Grave	2 (2 x 150)	3	Monday Wednesday Friday	Nijmegen, Emmerich, Duisburg, Neuss, Cologne, Mainz, Frankfurt, Mannheim, Karlsruhe
Rhinecontainer	Neptune Shipping	4 (4 x 200)	4	Monday (x2), Thursday, Friday	Bonn, Frankfurt, Mannheim, Wörth, Karlsruhe
CCS (Combined Container Service)	Rhenus Belgium	2 (2 x 208	2	Monday, Friday	Koblenz, Ginsheim
Frankenbach	Frankenbach (Rotterdam)		2	Tuesday, Friday	Mainz, Wörth
Alcotrans GVT	Haniel (Rotterdam), De Grave	5 (5 x 105)	3	Monday, Tuesday, Friday	Gernsheim, Strasbourg, Ottmarsheim, Basel
BCL (Basler Container Lloyd) CCS Dubbelman Häger und Schmidt	Rhenus Belgium RKE RKE	8 (3 x 208 + 93 + 99 + 105 + 111 + 192)	4	Monday, Tuesday Wednesday (x2)	Ludwigshafen, Mannheim, Wörth, Karlsruhe, Kehl, Strasbourg, Ottmarsheim, Weil, Basel, Birsfelden
CTG	CTG (Rotterdam)		2	Tuesday, Friday	Germersheim
Penta (Penta Container line AG) CFNR Natural Van Dam Conteba SRN	CFNR-Antwerpen RKE Neptune Shipping	6 (172 + 174 + 176 + 190 + 320 + 352)	3	Tuesday Wednesday Friday	Kehl, Strasbourg, Ottmarsheim, Weil, Basel

Source: Hinterland 164 (4/1995).

3.3.2 Close collaboration between maritime shippers and inland waterway carriers

In most cases, inland waterway carriers can provide their customers, who at present consist of maritime shippers or the agents of the latter, with a full chain of services based on the concept of combined transport. They can ensure both the positioning or haulage of empty containers and transportation from inland to maritime ports. They can even provide groupage/consignment splitting services, storage, warehousing and the repair of containers.

Maritime operators are no longer reluctant to use the inland waterways and most transport operations consist of carrier haulage, with the decline in the use of merchant haulage, and therefore act as sub-contractors, in some cases fully integrated, for maritime shippers.

Waterway operators group themselves together into pools or joint ventures. While this trend was initially observed in western Europe (see Table 16), groups of shippers have also emerged in the CEECs and, in most cases, consist of joint ventures with a partner from the West or the East. Such joint ventures allow groups to capitalise on their ability to work under different legal systems and means that they are no longer held back by the slow progress towards harmonization made by the various international commissions and the EU.

One example of such co-operation is that of the Elbe Container Line, a joint venture between *Deutsch Binnenreederei* in Berlin and the Czechoslovakian Elbe Shipping Co. (CSPL), which offers weekly sailings between Hamburg and Prague (700 km). This service offers transportation to the terminals at Magdeburg, Aken, Riesa, Dresden, Decin, Usti and Melnik.

These two companies are working together to prepare for the introduction of larger, river-borne container vessels on the Rhine. Since the late 1990s, shippers have been seeking ways to use larger vessels for the transport of containers as well as dangerous goods, in order to raise productivity. In 1994 the "Myriam" was constructed, a modular container barge 125.5 m long and 12.05 m wide, capable of carrying 232 TEU. Hitherto, barges operating on the Conventional Rhine and the Waal could be no more than 110 m long and 22.8 m wide, and the maximum authorised length of a push-towed convoy was 186.5 m. Since 1 October 1995, however, the central Commission for Navigation of the Rhine has authorised the operation of 135 m long self-propelled barges downstream of Mannheim. Work is therefore proceeding on the construction of a container barge 135 m long and 11.4 m wide, capable of transporting 272 TEU n a stack 17 units long, 4 units wide and 4 units deep, i.e. a carrying capacity equivalent to that of the Laurent-Laurens, a self-propelled push-towed two-barge unit, launched in 1987. This development reflects the trend towards larger vessels in the maritime sector.

At present, self-propelled barges 110 m long and 11.4 m wide are being operated on the Danube. These barges are capable of transporting 148 TEU stacked three containers high, from the Port of Komarno in Slovakia to the port of Deggendorf in Bavaria. In order to proceed towards Rotterdam via the Rhine-Main-Danube Canal, the top layer of containers must be unloaded due to insufficient clearance beneath three railway bridges which urgently need to be modified. This lack of competitiveness is considered to be unacceptable by all maritime and waterway shippers as well as the maritime ports.

The size of convoys is smaller in France. The vessels used on the Seine consist of a 1 200 hp push-towed unit and a Europa-type barge with a capacity of 60 TEU or, according to requirements, operators can use two 24-TEU barges or a single 60-TEU barge plus another 24-TEU barge, or even two 60-TEU capacity barges. Operators are keen to employ new techniques, such as modular vessels for mixed carriage of containers and dry bulk goods.

A major collaborative research effort, involving both maritime and inland waterway operators, has been undertaken in the Netherlands to seek ways of reducing handling costs. The latest of these techniques is that of self-loading container vessels for waterway transport. Like ocean-going vessels, inland waterway vessels can be fitted with the Kieboom transhipment hoist system.

This project is one of the lateral transhipment systems developed by J. Kieboom, who also developed the roller-barge. We shall probably see a massive return to the use of self-propelled barges in the form of self-loading vessels. This technique, once mastered, allows unimpeded lateral unloading. However, in the case of 40-foot containers, two cargo hoists are often essential.

3.3.3   *Role of maritime shippers*

Maritime shippers have a fundamental role to play. They approve river terminals and work with waterway charterers.

The creation of GIE Logiseine, a group made up of Paris Terminal (30 per cent), the Normandy terminals (30 per cent) at Le Havre and the *Compagnie Fluviale de Transport* (CFT) (40 per cent), was only possible with the support of the maritime shipper, Nedlloyd, working in association with Mitsui and the CMA.

120

Maritime shippers look set to increase their control over inland transport. Further to EU Directive 91/400, this trend, which is similar to the development of the landbridge, the minibridge and the microbridge in the EU, now extends to rail transport. At present, the inland waterways are no longer the sole mode concerned. There are now two major operators in the rail sector: ERS (European Rail Shuttle), a grouping of Dutch railways (NS Cargo), Nedlloyd, Sealand, P&O, the Maersk offshoot of NS Cargo and NDX for DBAG, NS Cargo and CSX Sealand. This may lead to greater complementarity between the two modes or to competition over services to the hinterland of ports located on the seaboard between Zeebrugge and Hamburg. ICF may become one of their sub-contractors. Construction of the Betuwe, the North-South Brenner line or the steel Rhine may, together with other priority projects, lead to competition with waterway transport. In this respect, there is a danger that deregulation might lead to slippage.

3.3.4   *Measures by companies to promote combined transport*

It is worth noting the exemplary action taken by the company, Osterreichische Wasserkombi, which has set itself the goal of optimising, by whatever means possible, combined transport operations between the Danube countries and the two ports of Antwerp and Rotterdam. The Bavarian port of Deggendorf is a central link in this chain. This is recognition that waterways are the most multimodal of the modes of transport.

CNC-Transports seem to want to pursue a similar policy, using the river port of Lille as a base. It is stepping up train services to Le Havre and is planning to operate a weekly direct rail service from Lille to Rotterdam and a river barge service from Dunkirk to Antwerp on behalf of GIE NCS.

3.3.5   *Transit forwarders*

Transit forwarders are developing river-borne combined transport operations throughout North-West Europe. In France, it is only now that the largest transit forwarders in the Ile de France region are starting to give serious consideration to the alternative offered by inland waterways. One-stop shopping and the emergence of Non Vessel Operator Common Carriers may also help to encourage demand for waterway transport.

3.3.6   Role of the inland river ports

In response to the changed economic climate, the public port authorities in Germany are setting an example by diversifying their activities in order to attract high-value traffic flows. The ports of Düsseldorf and Cologne are leading the way in this respect and this trend is starting to gain momentum.

Through a judicious policy of investment in terminals and the creation of combined transport centres, the ports are being transformed into genuine multimodal platforms. As a result of this policy, traffic flows are refocusing on general cargo.

The most remarkable example of adaptation in Europe would seem to be that of the port of Duisburg. This port, while maintaining its traditional role as a fast-growing sea port handling bulk materials, in order to boost growth in general goods, and notably container traffic, which grew by 20 per cent in 1995 (91 341 TEU), has set up a Freeport and a Combiport (the KMV-Centrum) which is currently expanding rapidly and which has vertical quays providing inland waterway links to the terminal. In addition, the port has another area known as the Distriport, a vast complex for freight collection and distribution integrated into continental transport chains.

These Rhine ports set an example for the whole of Europe and new inland terminals are being set up in the Netherlands, Belgium and even in France. River feeder systems are being developed on the Seine by the *Port Autonome de Paris*, on the Rhône in a joint initiative by the river ports and the CNR, and on the Nord/Pas-de-Calais network by the port of Lille.

In most cases, however, river terminals work in partnership with one or more maritime ports.

3.3.7   Role of the maritime port authorities

The Port of Rotterdam

In order to achieve a more balanced modal split, the port authority is diversifying its investments. It has set aside Gld 150 million for the development of new wharves and for the construction of a floating terminal, designed to help river container transport operators avoid having to supply too many terminals. The authority is also opening the Beerdam, which at present prevents river boats from gaining direct access to the terminals at Maasvlatke and is constructing a platform for direct transhipment between boats, lorries and railway wagons.

122

However, these investments are part of a multimodal development policy, in that the port of Rotterdam is also proceeding with the construction of a railway line dedicated solely to freight, the *Betuwelijn*, even though rail transport only accounts for 5 per cent of the port's modal split. It would seem that the port authorities foresee the integration of external costs and rapid growth in container traffic in the near future.

The Port of Antwerp

Both the infrastructure and superstructure of the port of Antwerp have been designed to promote the inland waterways. All the terminals have been equipped with special facilities for the loading and unloading of river-borne container vessels. The same is true of the Europe terminal, opened in 1991, as well as the future North Sea and left bank terminals. Antwerp expects to handle traffic flows of 6 to 8 million TEU by the year 2000. In overall terms, efforts still need to be made to improve handling facilities with regard to both handling costs and access to gantries reserved primarily for ocean-going vessels.

3.4. The determining role played by inland waterways at land/sea and sea/land interfaces

The partnership between the inland waterways and maritime ports can only grow stronger since inland waterways are the mode of transport which is the most reliable, the best mode for the transport of high-volume flows, the most economical, the most compatible with environmental concerns and, given the technological advances referred to earlier and still being developed, the most multimodal means of transport.

Use must be made of the inland waterways, together with other modes of surface or river-sea transport, for the pre- or post-carriage of maritime container traffic in Europe which, according to conservative estimates, is set to double to 36 million TEU or, according to optimistic forecasts, to 44.8 million TEU by the year 2000. By then, as a result of the Delta 2000-8 plan, Rotterdam should be handling some 9 million TEU. This traffic is expected to double between the year 2000 and 2010.

The major Benelux ports and, to a lesser extent, the German ports, have a particularly well developed hinterland in terms of wide-gauge inland waterway infrastructure:

- The Rhine waterway system (over 800 000 TEU in 1995 -- i.e. the volume of traffic forecast in 1990 for the year 2010) with over forty terminals, 32 of which are actually on the Rhine. Transport costs along this corridor are 15 to 20 per cent cheaper than by road, including door-to-door deliveries;
- The Escaut-Rhine link: 760 000 TEU in 1995;
- The Rhine-Main-Danube link for long-distance transportation. In 1995, inland waterway traffic on the Rhine-Main-Danube canal amounted to 9 230 TEU between the Benelux ports and Austria, compared with 2 300 TEU in 1993. The company promoting this traffic is the Austrian combined transport operator, Osterreichische Wasserkombi, which buys wholesale transport services from the two operators, Danube Container Service and Rhein-Donau Container Line, and retails these services to its customers;
- Completion of the German Project 17 will provide the final link in the network. It will open an East-West corridor to Poland and central Europe through the Ruhr and Mittellandkanal and, in doing so, will increase competition with German maritime ports, notably, Hamburg and Bremen, on the one hand and the Benelux ports on the other.

Short-haul container transport continues to grow, as shown by the success of the Antwerp-Lille, Liège, Meerhout and Logiseine links. Dutch operators consider that inland waterway transport is now competitive over distances as short as 140 km.

In view of these developments, while maritime infrastructure will obviously be a factor in the distribution of ocean-going container traffic between the different ports of North-West Europe in the twenty-first century, the main factor will be the availability of inland feeder links. Moreover, at a time when the inland transport industry will probably have managed to internalise its external costs, access to wide-gauge waterways will certainly prove to be a determining factor in the success of maritime ports. The ranking of the future Main European Maritime ports may well be determined by their ability to transfer their traffic flows onto inland waterways. The degree to which they will be able to do this will depend heavily upon the quality of services, the density of the wide-gauge inland waterway network in their hinterland and, above all, the existence of links between the local network and an international wide-gauge waterway network on which goods can be shipped for long distances without the need for transhipment and which offers competitive, interoperable distribution hubs.

The French ports would seem to be poorly placed to meet this future competition, given the lack of adequate inland waterway links. The port of Le Havre, despite plans to handle 6 000-TEU container ships in the medium term, is at a large disadvantage in the short term, given the new economic climate in Europe, in that it has no large-vessel inland waterway links to the European Economic Area. Improved rail links and consignment scheduling will not be able to offset this shortcoming in economic terms. Dunkirk offers some potential assets, but at present is no more than a minor port. Marseilles-Fos suffers from the same handicap, while the Rhône and Saône -- large, wide-gauge waterways -- are dead-ends.

The port authorities in the Benelux countries or Germany are alone in being able to operate deep into their hinterland. The choice made by maritime shippers as to which port to use will primarily depend upon the costs of managing inland container traffic flows.

The interdependency of river waterway and maritime transport operations is steadily increasing. There now exists a synergy, from which all the partners involved can benefit, between the containerised traffic handled by the maritime ports in North-West Europe and that handled by the waterways. In 1995 the volume of containerised traffic on the Rhine amounted to over 800 000 TEU and, on the European waterway network as a whole, to almost 1.5 million TEU. Even France reported some 100 000 TEU. Inland waterways are now the most multimodal form of transport available to port authorities and are capable of winning substantial market share from the road sector. The market share of the latter must never be allowed to rise to the 87 per cent forecast for 2010 by the International Union for Inland Navigation. The output achieved by operators on the Rhine is now common knowledge and all that now remains is for operators in other countries to follow suit.

4. FUTURE MARKETS

4.1. What will be the determining factors in future markets?

Growth in future markets will be determined by trends in international trade both in Europe and world-wide, trends in economic growth and demand, particularly demand from the 470 million consumers in the European Area, technical progress in the river and waterway transport sector, and the approach adopted by the various actors concerned.

4.1.1   Economic factors

Trends in world trade will play a determining role. The current strong growth in international trade is already starting to slow and is likely to decline further in the future. Growth in world trade amounted to 9.8 per cent in 1994, falling to 8.6 per cent in 1995. It seems likely that growth in world trade, which has averaged 5.5 per cent over the past 10 years, may begin to lose momentum and may well settle at around 5-6 per cent a year. Since 1990, the rate of growth in world trade has outpaced that in manufacturing output due to the high level of movements of semi-finished goods, particularly in CEECs, where wage costs are lower. The continuation or reversal of this process of relocation will also play a determining role in the development of inland and maritime shipping. Unless a social clause is introduced in the countries of the South, the trend towards relocation may well accelerate as new generations of post-Panamax container vessels are launched on the market.

Trade both within Europe and with areas outside Europe will play a fundamental role in shaping the future of the inland waterways in Europe. This role will be amplified by the growing integration of these economically complementary regions.

Growth in international trade may amount to no more than 2 to 3 per cent, unless reconstruction in eastern Europe helps to fuel it to higher levels. Internal demand is at a similar level. Demand for transport in the 15-Member EU should grow at a similar pace. Imports grew at a rate of over 7.5 per cent in 1995 (although they are slowing for the EU as a whole), notably in Germany, the United Kingdom, Italy (where they have been offset by higher imports from the Netherlands, Spain and Turkey). Growth in exports is lower than the world average due to a sharp decline in extra-regional exports. Exports are down sharply in Germany, which is refocusing its markets, and the United Kingdom, but are growing at a rate of over 10 per cent in Italy and Austria. Intra-regional trade is growing faster than extra-regional trade. Two-thirds of the total volume of trade is within the Community area, which explains the size of flows. Demand for goods transport will probably continue to grow at an average rate of at least 1.5 per cent a year.

Over the same period, the rate of growth in exports from CEECs was higher than the world average for the third year running, although imports grew at a slower pace than exports. This higher rate of growth observed within Europe as a whole reflects the progress achieved in the transition process. Goods transport in the CEECs should grow strongly as a result of annual rates of growth, which in some corridors were as high as 33 per cent. The rate of growth should subsequently decline to a nonetheless buoyant level of 15-20 per cent.

Table 17. **Growth in value of world trade in goods by region 1990-95 ($ billion)**

| | Exports (FAB) | | | | Imports (CAF) | | | |
| | Value | Annual change | | | Value | Annual change | | |
	1995	1994	1995	90-95	1995	1994	1995	90-95
Western Europe	2 184	13%	21.5%	6%	2 178	11.5%	22%	5%
European Union	1 021	13%	22%	6%	2 008	12%	21%	5.5%
Central & Eastern Europe	68	20.5%	25%	8%	86	13%	27.5%	12.5%

Source: WTO.

In 1996, began a new stage in the economic transition of the Central European Free Trade Area (CEFTA) countries (including Roumania since 1997 – Visegrad Group).   During the first half of the year, exports to market-economy countries declined and there was renewed growth in trade with the Baltic States and the Community of Independent States (CIS); intra-regional trade also began to grow. The largest share of trade still remains that with the EU, however, which accounts for 60 per cent of all trade flows. Germany, at 26 per cent, accounts for the largest share of such trade and is the largest trading partner of all the CEECs apart from Bulgaria, whose largest trading partner is Russia. Italy accounts for 40 per cent of Albanian trade. These two EU Member States are by far the largest trading partners of the CEFTA countries.

Poland, the Czech Republic and Slovakia played a major role in the reorganisation of trade patterns. Exports from these three countries to the Baltic States have grown astoundingly quickly, rising by 40 per cent -- and even 70 per cent in some cases -- during the first half of 1996. There has also been spectacular growth of between 20 and 40 per cent in trade to CIS countries. Hungary, Bulgaria and Romania, however, were exceptions to this trend. Intra-regional trade between CEFTA countries rose from 6 to 10 per cent (excluding bilateral trade between Slovakia and the Czech Republic).

Trade between eastern Europe and the developing countries has also risen at a rate second only to that in trade with the Baltic States and the CIS. Exports to the developing countries from Hungary, the Czech Republic and Poland have risen by 15-20 per cent. Imports from the developing countries to Romania have risen from 25-35 per cent. Romania is the only country to which exports from this area have risen. The overall share of the developing countries in trade with eastern European countries remains modest, however, accounting for only 8 per cent of exports and 7 per cent of imports.

The breakdown of products in value terms for the first half of 1996 shows that chemicals, machinery, transport equipment and manufactured goods account for a large share of the exports from CEFTA countries (excluding Slovenia): 81 per cent of exports and 46.8 per cent of imports. The latter are now declining. This trend reflects the initial impacts of the output from the local affiliates of western companies that are now supplying local markets and re-exporting a share of their output from those countries. This would account for part of the massive increase in trade flows to the Baltic States and the CIS. The growing share of the latter is attributable to an increase in imports of energy products and an increase in exports of basic manufactured goods. Agricultural and agro-food products account for over 10 per cent of exports from the CEECs as a whole, except for the Czech Republic, Slovakia and Slovenia. A new pattern of more diversified flows would therefore seem to be emerging. The East-West oriented flows remain dominant, although flows are starting to re-emerge along corridors oriented more or less North-South or South-West/North-East. Trade to and from the Mediterranean region, the Middle East and Suez is starting to grow.

In 1990, the firm PROGNOS forecast that by the year 2000 the value of imports to the West from the East would grow by a factor of 10 and that the value of exports from the West to the East would grow by a factor of 13.

East-West trade in terms of the volume of goods transported has apparently risen by a factor of 4.4, an average annual growth rate of 14 per cent over the period 1989-2000. This growth looks set to continue and, by the year 2000, per capita exports from these countries should reach the level observed in western European countries in 1980. These forecasts are now becoming reality, and indeed the rate of growth would actually seem to be slightly higher than predicted.

Imports from the West are growing at a rate of 30 per cent, except in the case of Hungary, and exports from eastern European countries at a rate of 7-10 per cent. However, the economic "catching-up" process is far from over and it should be noted that the per capita wealth of all the CEECs combined is 10 times less than that of Germany.

The geographical origin of investments also has an important role to play. The scale of the inflow of German capital tends to encourage trade flows towards Germany, although German investment may also use this area as a hub for directing flows towards the Baltic States, the CIS, Russia and the Middle East, in the same way that inflows of capital from the Far East (Japan, Korea) and South-East Asia (Singapore) can generate trade flows to or from those regions.

Market growth is also linked to the speed and quality of restructuring. Major differences in this respect are to be seen between Poland, for example, and Bulgaria which only began to emerge from its recessionary spiral in 1994.

There is scope for substantial growth in transit traffic in Bulgaria, which occupies a key geographical position on the boundary between the West and the Slav countries of the East. This explains the size of Bulgaria's trade flows in 1994 with Russia and the CIS: 17.6 per cent of all exports and 26.6 per cent of imports. The effect of geographical proximity is also apparent in Greece and Turkey. The embargo on the former Yugoslavia, however, left Bulgaria locked into a Balkan enclave by sharply curbing transport flows to that country, particularly on the Danube. However, the share of exports from the OECD area rose from 12 per cent to 38 per cent over the period 1991 to 1994 and the share of imports from 20 per cent to 49 per cent. In addition, numerous foreign companies, such as Coca-Cola, Nestlé, Rover, etc., have invested in the country.

The Hungarian approach appears to be one of the success stories of the transition process. The Hungarian economy began to grow strongly in 1994. From 1993 onwards, industrial output started to grow at an annual rate of 4 per cent, accelerating in 1994 to 9.2 per cent. In 1995, output grew by 11 per cent and exports by over 20 per cent. Hungarian exports only began to increase in volume terms in 1994, when they rose by 12.1 per cent. In 1995, this growth amounted to 11 per cent in value terms as a result of the improved economic climate in the West. Demand in the OECD area for Hungarian goods apparently rose by 6 per cent in 1994 and by 5.5 per cent in 1995. The problems that the economy would now seem to be facing are those of inadequate domestic demand and lack of demand for Hungarian unfinished goods and spare parts.

The Romanian economy seems to have been revitalised by the private sector and by a slow recovery in agricultural output. The economy started to recover in late 1993 and subsequently grew strongly in 1994 and 1995. Romania has redirected its trade flows towards OECD Member countries, an area which accounted for 48 per cent of its exports and 57 per cent of its imports, 80 per cent of which were with EU Member States. The leading destinations for Romanian exports are Germany, Italy and France; the main sources of Romanian imports are Germany, Russia, Italy, the EU and France.

The first of the countries in transition to recover was Poland, whose economy grew by 1 per cent in 1992 and by 4.5 per cent in 1993. Over the same period, industrial output rose by 4.2 per cent to reach 10 per cent by the end of 1993.

The Czech Republic has made a "miraculous" recovery. The economy started to grow strongly from 1993 onwards. GDP grew by 3 per cent in 1994 and by 4 per cent in 1995. Slovakia's economy also began to recover in 1994, although demand remains slack.

Slovenia's GDP began to grow again in 1993, a trend confirmed in 1995 and 1996 with growth rates of 4.5 per cent. External trade has been redirected towards western European countries, which by the end of 1994 accounted for 72.6 per cent of Slovenia's exports and 78 per cent of imports. Germany is Slovenia's leading trade partner for both exports and imports, followed by Italy and then Austria. Intra-regional trade with other Republics of the former Yugoslavia has collapsed and accounts for no more than 8 per cent of a diversified industrial fabric served by a relatively dense network of infrastructure.

4.1.2   Trends in economic output

The agricultural output of western Europe should level off and may even start to decline as a result of new European regulations on the use of inputs. The environmental crisis in the countryside should lead to a decline in output of cereals and agricultural output in general. New crops may emerge as a result of advances in the production of hybrids such as soya.

However, this decline will probably be offset by increased productivity in central and eastern Europe. In Hungary, agriculture now makes a substantial contribution to foreign trade and the agro-food industry accounts for 20 per cent of exports and 7 per cent of imports. In Bulgaria, the agricultural sector produces major export items such as vegetables, wine, tobacco and citrus fruits. Slovenia now has a prosperous agricultural industry. Romania and Poland have once again started to export agricultural produce.

The trend towards industrial relocation in western Europe will continue in the refining sector, which is increasingly transferring operations to producer countries. Over the next few years, major industrial sites will undergo extensive restructuring, particularly at locations such as the Rhône Valley in France and Pernis in the Netherlands. This should not, however, have an impact on waterway traffic, which has already been severely affected.

Other sectors of industry that exploit advanced technologies, such as specialty steel production, ceramics and machine-tools, should remain in place. One of the main prerequisites for maintaining such activities is the existence of efficient inland transport chains.

In CEECs, activities in the refining sector are being restructured and upgraded. Current installed capacities are too small and outmoded to meet future requirements. These countries are therefore experiencing renewed industrial specialisation and diversification.

Romania's energy requirements necessitate the importation of at least 12-13 million tonnes of oil a year. There are three major industrial sectors, namely, chemicals, petrochemicals and electronics. The industrial sector is diversifying as a result of foreign investment not only from Europe but also from East and South-East Asia. Daewoo has played a major role in these changes.

In Hungary, the mining industry is declining. There has been sustained growth in the agro-food and textile/clothing industries, although the strongest growth has been in the metal-working and metallurgical industries. Between them, the latter two sectors accounted for 44 per cent of Hungary's exports of industrial goods in 1995 and, in value terms, this flow has increased by over 27 per cent. Production of household appliances is also growing strongly. The number of suppliers to the car industry to have set up plants in Hungary has grown sharply: General Motors (engines and vehicle assembly), Audi (engines), Ford (parts) and Suzuki (assembly).

Firms which have set up plants in the Czech Republic include Volkswagen, Procter and Gamble, the Belgian glass-making firm, Glaverbel, Danone, ASEA, Mercedes-Benz and a large number of firms in the petrochemical and telecommunications sectors.

Poland and Slovenia both have diversified economies.

Logistical and distribution activities are growing strongly in all areas and the trade flows they generate offer potential market share for the inland waterways.

4.1.3   *Trends in inland waterway and maritime shipping techniques*

There have been some spectacular technological advances in the maritime shipping sector.

The collapse of the freight shipping market between 1982 and 1986 allowed firms to relocate and accelerated the globalisation of markets already in progress. The maritime shipping industry reverted to the use of mega-vessels. Within ten years, the average capacity of container ships operating on East-West lines had increased from 3 000 to 3 500 TEU, after which the trend accelerated. The last orders placed by P&O are for vessels with a capacity of 6 700 TEU. Current forecasts indicate that this trend will be maintained in the future and will help bring about a dramatic reduction in transport costs. It is projected that future vessels will have a capacity of 8 000, 10 000, 12 000 and 18 000 TEU.

Shipping distances are becoming increasingly immaterial and are declining faster than in the inland sector. Shipping costs per kilometre, for example, have fallen dramatically. The projected shipping costs for container vessels are as follows:

> 6 000-TEU vessel = 400 dollars/TEU   (Antwerp/Hong Kong or Singapore)
> 8 000-TEU vessel = 250 dollars/TEU
> 10 000-TEU vessel = 158 dollars/TEU
> 15 000-TEU vessel = 80-100 dollars/TEU.

In comparison, the per-kilometre costs for carrying a consignment by land from Antwerp to Lille or from Le Havre to Paris are exorbitant. Only the inland waterways are capable of competing with such costs. At all events, combined transport will need to be used.

The use of inland waterways is also dictated by the size of freight flows: to transport the freight carried by a 6 000-TEU container ship requires a convoy of lorries, spaced at the requisite regulatory interval, 200 km long or 2 000 wagons (i.e. 80 trains), but only fifteen convoys of container barges carrying 400 TEU each. Another question arises at this point. Below the 250 dollar mark, how many European industries, other than high-tech sectors, will be able to compete? Perhaps some flows might simply disappear?

Another surprising revolution has taken place in the energy sector. A specialised vessel capable of transporting hydrogen has recently been launched in Germany, presumably as part of that country's energy plans for the twenty-first century.

However, the draught of these vessels limits the number of ports that they can use. The "Regina Maersk", the first generation of such vessels, measures 318 m long, 42 m wide and has a draught of 14 m.

These developments are not only redrawing the map of shipping flows and creating a new league table of ports with sufficient deep water berths, they are also creating a climate of keen competition for cheap, high-capacity inland transport services that are not environmentally damaging. The inland waterways are capable of meeting these criteria.

The vessels used for inland navigation are constantly evolving to meet the needs of maritime shippers: modular self-propelled barges, self-loading, self-propelled barges, increasingly powerful self-propelled push-tug barges.

The trend is therefore towards the construction of vessels that are 20 to 25 per cent lighter with a shallower draught. These vessels are 110 m long and 11.45 m wide and suitable for navigation on the Rhine and the Danube.

The EU and other international bodies must encourage these changes in fleet composition and the ability of fleets to supply efficient vessels with a higher degree of autonomy with regard to loading and unloading.

4.1.4   Developments in infrastructure and superstructure in the inland waterway sector

In order to meet the new requirements of shippers and charterers, the inland waterway transport sector must be able to supply high-quality services. This calls for a network of wide inland waterways and inland ports which can operate as proper multimodal platforms with faultless logistical services.

Which network would be suitable?

The UN/ECE network would seem to be the best. Its geographical layout meets all of the economic and environmental requirements of the European continent. This uniform network is suitable for use by standard units (self-propelled barges, push-towed convoys) and is widely accessible to ocean-going vessels. For the first time, standard dimensions have been listed in a regulatory text. The AGN aims to increase the market share of waterway transport, which is cheap, efficient and perfectly compatible with the environment, in all international trade flows. This network strengthens the economic co-operation between countries in both eastern and western Europe. The AGN sets out a network of inland waterways of international importance (E-ways). These waterways link major maritime ports and coastal routes with the hinterland. They offer outlets to the Channel coasts, the North Sea, the Baltic and the White Sea, as well as to the coasts of the Mediterranean, the Black Sea and the Caspian Sea. The northernmost and southernmost corridors are coastal maritime routes surrounding the European continent from the White Sea to the Caspian Sea. These routes necessitate the use of river/maritime traffic and short-sea crossings. The E-way network stretches from the Atlantic Ocean to the Urals, linking 37 countries and providing access to areas outside Europe.

This network does not yet properly meet demand. It seems to take no account of the request made periodically by the Austrian Government for the go-ahead to be given to the construction of the Danube/Oder Canal. For Austria, this canal offers a solution to the problem of transit traffic by road from which this country is likely to suffer increasingly. North-South trade flows are growing larger. The construction of the canal would allow energy savings to be made and would offer efficient surface transport costs. Trade flows between Poland, the Czech Republic and the Slovak Republic would thus increase, as they would along the entire Danube. At current prices, the CCI in Vienna estimates that construction of the 290 km long canal would cost Sch 25 billion (FF 12 billion). The construction of this link would also help the development of a number of Baltic ports, such as Swinoujscie, upstream of Szczecin, which can accommodate draughts of 13 m. The first and most important step would seem to be to implement the proposals put forward by the European Commission [COM(92) 231/7].

The development of a network of infrastructure, harmonization of canal gauges and access conditions, would have a dramatic impact on the market.

Table 18. Development of inland waterway services in countries with a waterway network

	Inland waterway network (in km)		Inland waterway traffic (in t-km billions)		Trends in traffic
	1970	1994	1970	1994	1970-94
France	7 433	7 376	14.2	5.6	-61%
Germany	4 508	6 958*	48.8	61.8**	+23%
Netherlands	5 999	5 046	30.7	36.1	+18%
Belgium	1 553	1 513	6.7	5.5	-18%

*   After reunification.
**   Including 2 billion t/km in the former GDR.
Source: Eurostat.

The situation of the inland waterway sector in France contrasts sharply with that in Germany. Between 1975 and 1984, Germany invested three times as much as France in the inland waterway sector, excluding investment by semi-public firms. The total volume of waterway traffic in Germany amounts to 61.8 billion t/km, three times that in France. The average length of trip on the inland waterways in France is 112 km, compared with 213 km in Germany. The lack of interconnections between river basins and the disparate nature of the French inland waterway network explains this difference. Average productivity measured in terms of t/km per boat is therefore lower in France, where it amounts to 1.3 compared with 14 in Germany. The limited number of wide-gauge waterways, which account for scarcely 21 per cent of the network excluding estuaries, and the lack of mobility of most of the more modern fleets explain this poor performance. Most charterers surveyed in the Paris Region stated that they were unfamiliar with this mode of transport. In some cases, they share facilities with the mode without making use of it. For such operators, the waterways are still a vestige of the past. For many years, this mode has not been properly promoted and its commercial techniques are outmoded.

The transport supply on the Lille to Paris route, which on some sections is restricted to 750 tonnes (theoretically 990 tonnes, but this tonnage is impossible in reality), is such that operators are often discouraged from making use of it. Use of this route requires costly transhipment and pre- and post-carriage, usually by road, and the potential savings compared with road transport are therefore low. However, a convoy made up of a self-propelled barge and a push-towed barge can transport between 1 500 and 1 800 tonnes. On the Paris-Strasbourg route, on which the gauge is limited to 399 tonnes, the potential benefits offered by the waterways will be cancelled out if charterers are not located at sites which have moorings. To disregard the inland waterways as a mode of transport is a mistake. In the Lille-Paris corridor, the volume of road traffic is expected to increase to 20 000 lorries a day by the year 2005 according to official forecasts, but will probably amount to far more in the light of the dramatic growth in containerised traffic which studies, carried out by Fearnley's for the Benelux ports, predict is likely to be experienced up to the years 2005 and 2010. The maximum carrying capacity of a single motorway lane before it is saturated amounts to 13 000 lorries a day and the A1 motorway is already approaching this limit, hence the urgent need to construct the Seine-Nord canal.

New waterways must be of high quality and must meet minimum technical requirements.

In the short term, the major inland waterways must be able to accommodate convoys of at least Class IV, which would thus allow full integration of the European area through the waterway network. Both on environmental grounds and because of the need to increase the accessibility of ports on the Baltic Sea and the Black Sea, the inland waterway network will be called upon to play a determining role in trade flows. Corridors with the highest traffic densities should be upgraded to Class Va. In order to promote containerised traffic, there must be at least 7 m of water depth available in waterways. Ideally, this depth should be increased to 9 m to allow containers to be stacked four-high. Locks should be manned, and navigation should be permitted twenty-four hours a day.

Combined transport infrastructure must meet the technical standards set out in the AGTC agreement drawn up by the UN/ECE in order to ensure that multimodal transport is efficient.

River terminals must have excellent land links to ensure their accessibility, which will require the planning of infrastructure for the inland waterways, road and rail to be properly co-ordinated. River ports must be platforms for at least three modes of transport and preferably four, five or, in the case of the most efficient ports, six modes. The superstructure of such ports must be such that the impact of transhipment is minimised. The modernisation of ports on the Danube is therefore a matter of some urgency.

The EU must encourage the governments of all countries, and particularly those in CEECs, to which it provides international aid, to offer incentives to firms to relocate to sites with access to waterways. Governments should do this either by providing tax breaks or by creating free areas, particularly in view of the fact that most of the trade by these firms is with Germany, Italy and Austria.

By the same token, the EU should also promote combined transport. It is essential to carry out the following work to ensure waterway networks are properly integrated into existing plans:

–   The dredging of the Elbe, approved in December 1997, in order to increase draught clearance; extension of the port at Altenwerder; and above all the dredging and deepening of the Elbe between Magdeburg and the Czech border;

–   Inter-network connections: construction of missing links such as introduction of standard gauges on the Elbe-Oder link which has the potential to accommodate large flows of traffic. Despite the mediocre nature of present waterways, the volume of international freight transported on this canal amounts to 2.8 million tonnes. Most of the trade concerns eastern Germany, with Berlin accounting for 80 per cent of the traffic. The traffic flows out of eastern Germany consist of coal, coke, gravel, cement, iron, steel and chemical products. Some of this traffic is directed towards France: chemical products to Mortagne; lead concentrates to Noyelles-Godault; coiled steel to Dunkirk or Lille; copper from Wroclaw to the Ardennes. In such cases, the freight is routed via Liège-Monsin. Goods transported into eastern Germany include fertilisers, iron and steel products, chemicals, kaolin and machinery. Building interconnections between isolated wide waterway networks, which are under-utilised within the European area, is a priority, as is the upgrading of existing waterways. In France, interconnections should be built between the Seine and the northern network, the Rhine and the Rhône and the Seine and the eastern network; in addition, work should continue on construction of a link between the northern network in France and the Belgian network. In Poland, a link should be built between the Vistula and the Oder. As part of the continuing upgrading of the Mittellandkanal, plans have been made to construct a new 900 km waterway running East-West from Koszalin to Brest-Litovsk via Warsaw. This will be the Oder-Warta-Vistula-Bug link;

–   Elimination of bottlenecks. The bridges on the Rhine-Main-Danube Canal must rapidly be raised. On the German section of the Danube, the problem of inadequate water depth must be solved. The navigability of the entire Danube needs to be studied and improved. The contract signed by the EU to carry out an in-depth study of the Danube must be implemented. By the year 2005-2010, the volume of traffic along the entire length of the Danube corridor will exceed the current volume of transit traffic through the Alps. The nominal capacities of the Danube are currently under-utilised for political reasons, but also because of technical shortcomings. The Danube must be transformed into a key component of the transport infrastructure for traffic flows between East and West, and to do this it is necessary to:

- improve the navigability and technical capacities of the Danube;
- restructure fleets and adapt their capacity to current market requirements;
- modernise existing port infrastructure, build new ports, use ports as the hubs of transport chains;
- ensure proper interoperability between the navigable waterways of eastern and western Europe.

The potential economic and environmental benefits are enormous. However, improvement of waterways must not be driven solely by transport markets but must also be part of an integrated development policy for the European area.

Feasibility studies of projects and their potential benefits address issues such as current and potential demand, domestic (local, interregional, national) and international trade, the versatility of waterways and many socio-economic aspects such as access to remote regions. Development of the Danube corridor, now that peace has returned to the region, can help to promote regional integration and foster new synergies. In the long term, the Danube will become, like the Rhine corridor, one of the major and determining corridors in the European area. It will restore the balance of the "blue banana", in the same way that the Seine-Rhône corridor could if the Rhine-Rhône link were to be built.

Passenger transport is another aspect that should be taken into consideration. Tourism, which is already well developed on the Rhine, is currently a growth market. Cruises on the Danube or between the North Sea and the Black Sea and the Mediterranean offer similar potential for growth, as do cruises between the Baltic and the Black Sea.

The eastwards expansion of the European Union which has now been decided will offer Europe a new market of 110 million people, leading to investment, infrastructure development, consumption and growth.

In the longer term, the future development of the Polish ports is inevitable, despite their limited accessibility due to the shallow depth of the Kattegat (-13m). These ports are relatively ice-free, unlike the ports in the Baltic States, and the depth of their harbours (-15 m in Swinoujscie, -13 m in Gdynia and -10 m in Gdansk) can accommodate ships with a capacity of 3 000 to 3 500 TEU. Without wishing to offend the port authorities of Rotterdam or

Hamburg, the development of these ports would restore the balance of continental traffic flows and would amply justify the construction of the Vistula-Dnieper link.

This development work must be carried out in accordance with bilateral and multilateral international agreements between the EEC and the countries in transition and the EEC and transit countries. They are all included in European plans and international agreements (AGN, AGTC).

However, it is unfortunate that the PACT programme (Pilot Action for Combined Transport -- 1992-2000) attached such little importance to inland waterways. Of the 22 routes covered by the programme, only three were by inland waterway: between the Netherlands (Rotterdam) and Austria (Vienna); between Rotterdam and Basel; between Rotterdam and Antwerp and between Rotterdam and Lille. Why not include the East-West corridor?

A highly competitive inland waterway offering high-quality services cannot but be accepted by a general public that is increasingly concerned over protection of the environment and safety. Such a waterway calls for high-quality improvement work. One example of this is the Rhine-Main-Danube Canal.

4.1.5   *Trends in maritime transport flows and the geographical distribution of flows*

Trends in maritime traffic

In Europe, while coal transport can be expected to grow, there is unlikely to be dramatic growth in the transport of oil and dry bulk goods. Indeed, flows of the latter two goods are likely to decline at an average rate of 2-4 per cent a year unless there is a dramatic recovery in the economy and, even if there were growth, would still remain limited to 5 per cent. In contrast, flows of manufactured goods will continue to grow strongly at a rate of at least 4-6 per cent a year and perhaps even as high as 10 per cent. Average GDP in the OECD area is only expected to grow by 2.5 per cent over the next few years, while industrial output in Europe, fuelled by reconstruction in central and eastern Europe, is forecast to grow at a rate of 3 per cent, higher than the average in the OECD area. OECD experts and Norwegian brokers are unanimous on this point.

We can expect to see dramatic growth in containerised traffic (*source:* Ocean Shipping Consultants). The outlook for container traffic at the world level is as follows:

Year	TEU millions
1977	22.00
1980	36.35
1994	127.54
1995	141.00
2000	222.30
2005	306 (conservative assumption) 335 (optimistic assumption)

2010	391(conservative assumption of 335 km of new quayside
	    frontage and 1 200 new gantry cranes)
	465(optimistic assumption of 480 km of new quayside frontage;
	    8 000-TEU container vessels, i.e. super-Panamax; and
	    1 800 gantry cranes to be installed at terminals

The regional breakdown of traffic reflects the unevenness of economic growth world-wide and the impact of globalisation and the attendant transfers of industrial activities. While the volume of container traffic to and from North-East and South-East Asia has soared, containerised traffic in Europe is also growing strongly despite gradually losing market share for such traffic.

Containerised traffic in Europe:

Year	TEU millions	Share of world traffic
1980	11.49	31.6%
1995	33.06	23.3
2000	44.80	
2010	87.00 80.90	18.7% (conservative scenario) 20.7% (optimistic scenario)

According to US studies, bulk imports to eastern Europe, despite the recession that has affected this region, should grow by 10 per cent in the course of the 1990s. Overall tonnages of international trade in this area are expected to rise from 536 million tonnes to 602 million tonnes by around the year 2000.

Containerised traffic is forecast to grow as follows (figures in TEU thousands):

	1997	1998	1999	2000
Bulgaria	51.0	53.1	55.5	58.0
Czech Republic	5.3	5.5	5.8	6.2
Hungary	17.0	18.0	19.1	20.2
East Germany	162.7	173.2	184.5	197.4
Poland	164.9	175.7	186.2	199.2
Romania	38.9	40.5	42.3	44.2
CIS	160.8	164.9	169.8	174.9

Rotterdam, Antwerp, Hamburg, Felixstowe, Zeebrugge, and possibly in time, Le Havre for containerised traffic, will become the future Main Ports of Europe, offering the best berthing facilities to mega-carriers. These are the ports whose scheduled connecting inland transport services have the greatest capacity and are the most competitive, serving a densely populated hinterland and enjoying efficient feeder links. These links are of such importance to shippers that the latter are increasingly tempted to secure control over them through consortia such as NDX, CSX (Maersk) and eventually Hanjin.

This policy has prompted shippers operating in the Mediterranean to sideline the port of Marseilles because of its negative image, the absence of a well-served hinterland, and the fact that the Rhône waterway network has no connections to other waterways.

The formation of "mega-alliances" encourages major operators to concentrate flows to a given market, for example, the European market, within a limited number of ports per geographical area and to concentrate their land-based logistics operations in order to achieve economies of scale. The ports chosen therefore become Main Ports, hubs for mother ships, while other ports find themselves given a minor role to play in serving feeders or small transhipment vessels. At present, there are twenty Main Ports worldwide, of which three are in Europe (Rotterdam, Hamburg and Antwerp). Le Havre is ranked in 54th position!

In the competition for trade, North-West Europe handles 72 per cent of all European containerised traffic, compared with 28 per cent handled by Mediterranean ports. The larger the ship, the more certain ports are relegated to the sidelines. To qualify as a direct destination, a port must be able to accommodate 15 per cent of the carrying capacity of the ship, i.e. 500 containers for a ten-year old ship, but 1 000 containers for a mega-container vessel of the latest generation.

In addition, the emergence of ports specialised in logistics and distribution in the Mediterranean area is taking trade away from merchant ports such as Marseilles in their own catchment area. Examples of such dynamic ports include Barcelona, Algeçiras, Marsaxlokk (Malta) and Cagliari (Tauro). These ports are typical examples of hub ports located on a strategic route. Lacking an immediate hinterland, they all have one advantage in common -- they are all located along the Gibraltar-Suez route. They are specialised in the collection and redistribution through feeder networks of container flows to and from merchant ports. These ports also have the advantage of requiring little deviation from routes and extremely low transhipment costs owing to currency parities and highly favourable labour costs. Cyprus thus serves as a feeder port for the Black Sea ports, until such time as the latter decide to modernise their facilities. The next generation of container ships (8 000-TEU capacity) could not at present be accommodated by any of the Black Sea ports owing to lack of sufficient water depth. Only the ports of Sulina (-13 to 15 m) and Odessa (-19 m) are capable of accommodating 6 000-TEU container ships. The other ports on the Black Sea coast, Burgas (-12.8 m), Constanta (-12 m), Drozba (-11 m) and Iljicovsk (-12.6 m) can accommodate 3 000 to 3 500-TEU vessels. Special consideration should be given to the port of Midia, located at the point where the Danube Canal reaches the Black Sea. If full advantage is to be taken of the trend towards mega-vessels, then an intermediate solution might be to construct a major terminal at Thessalonika, after deepening the channel, since the current depth of water is merely -13 m, and then to put in place waterway feeders to the Danube countries until a canal is built between this port and the Danube. The Danube is accessible to large coasters as far upstream as Turnu-Severin (3.7 m), except during the low-water season between August and December when sometimes there are not enough moorings available. Sea-going vessels cannot go any further than Braila. The ports currently in difficulty on this section of the Danube must transform themselves into multimodal platforms in order to gain a new lease of life. The Delta ports (Tulcea, Izmail, Isaccea, Reni, Galati, Braila, Kilija, etc.) have water depths of 7-8.5 m and are all advance outposts on the edge of this economic area, which was formerly very active and which must once again become prosperous. The Lunaa or Balta (major channel of the Danube) has no fewer than ten cities which are all highly industrialised ports whose infrastructure is simply crying out to be modernised and revitalised. Some of this work will have to be carried out in co-operation with Bulgaria. Nine ports are located at potential sites for cross-border hubs: Calarasi-Silistra, Oltenita-Tutrakan, Giurgu-Ruse, Zimnicea-Svistov, Turnu Magurele-Nikopol, Corabia, Bechet-Orjahovo, Lom, Vidin-Calafat. Traffic flows are currently extremely low on this section of the Danube and non-existent, or almost so, on the Danube-Black Sea Canal. The upgrading of Hungarian ports currently in progress (Györ, Budapest, Dunaujvaros, Baja, Szeged, Szekszard), with the aim of giving each port a transhipment capacity of from 1 to 3 million tonnes, holds out hope of a revival of this major corridor. The dramatic increase in traffic through Budapest and the Slovakian port of Komarno should help to fuel such a revival. In the medium-term, development of the Danube corridor should help to slow the growth in transit traffic through Germany and the Rhine corridor and allow efficient, transshipment-free links to be put in place between the Danube countries, the CIS and the Middle East. The port of Genoa might also be used to handle transit freight traffic to and from the countries of the former Yugoslavia. This would help create a synergy within the region that would be beneficial in human, economic and environmental terms.

The medium term might also see the emergence of a new North-South corridor that would reduce the length of continental legs and that would spare the Netherlands or Germany further increases in transit traffic. The precondition for such a change would be a shift of trade flows in the Baltic Sea. Over the past three years, feeder and inland waterway operators have prospered in this area as a result of partnership agreements between the major ports in the Rhine delta, notably Rotterdam, and the Baltic ports and Riga in particular. However, ships with a draught of 13 m, such as 3 000 to 3 500-TEU container ships, are capable of navigating through the Kattegat and of reaching the ports of Swinoujscie, Gdynia and, once upgraded, Rostock. The first two locations should be given priority by virtue of their land links. Both offer scope for the development of river-borne combined transport operations. The benefits for Poland of such a development would be an inflow of foreign currency and the revitalisation of its business sector, fuelled by greater access to overseas markets.

Such a development, however, will clearly depend upon the attitude of the actors concerned and upon whether they are willing to direct investment where it is needed; it cannot happen spontaneously.

4.1.6   The attitude of actors

International organisations, the EU and governments, as well as port authorities, carriers and shippers, all have a crucial role to play in the development process.

The approach of governments and international organisations

To take account of the objectives of the UN/ECE, which are to harmonize networks and promote intermodality in the interest of safeguarding the environment, will require governments, at least with regard to CEECs, to provide aid for the reconstruction of those countries' inland waterways; that is to say, governments will have to secure funding from the BIRD or the BERD or to encourage private international investment.

Although in signing the AGN, governments have committed themselves to developing their waterway infrastructure of international importance in accordance with the conditions of the agreement, they still need to provide the funding for such work.

The UN/ECE and the ECMT must ensure that their inland infrastructure develop programmes are consistent in order to safeguard the environment and achieve a balanced modal split.

This will require governments to consider the breakdown of investment funding by mode. It is clear, however, that there are major distortions in this area, even within western European countries.

The future policies of both governments and the EU must give priority to intermodal complementarity and must seek to avoid encouraging competition that would be disastrous for all modes. Policies must promote combined waterway transport and combined waterway and maritime transport in order to reduce external costs. In the case of large urban areas, the use of waterways for passenger transport is one way to combat air pollution. Regional development policy at both the national and the international level must focus on the versatility of inland waterways. Tax incentives and other measures should be used to encourage industry or logistics operators to locate their activities at sites along major waterway arteries. Secondary corridors can also be used to stimulate activities in the regions they cross; a shipment made by a Freycinet barge can be competitive provided that the trip is between two firms with premises alongside the waterway. The inland waterways can help to foster growth in tourism, particularly eco-tourism, by means of combined waterway/sea cruises. A number of governments have met with success in this area (Netherlands, United Kingdom, Germany, Belgium, etc.), and there is greater potential for development in this area in France, Italy and central and eastern Europe. The major river corridors, the Rhine and the Danube, have enormous potential markets.

It has taken far too long, however, to put a European policy in place. Many difficulties have held back the policy process at the European level. The legacy of networks and policies inherited from the past has left outmoded transport organisational structures in each of the Member countries and has slowed the process of harmonization. A radical overhaul is needed but the potential impact of such action, in some cases because of the technical nature of the operation, is causing governments to hesitate. In addition, there are historical, structural and political obstacles. Furthermore, governments have always tended to associate transport with strategy and therefore would rather keep decisionmaking powers within their own jurisdiction. As a result, transport policy at the European level remained in an embryonic state until 1985, thus holding back the economic construction of Europe. European transport policy lacks the resources needed to implement it, a problem that has been compounded by the reactions of governments insistent on retaining their sovereignty. The EU has repeatedly encountered problems in its attempts to eliminate national discrimination and to draw up common rules. With regard to inland waterway policy, the EU is faced with differences of opinion between governments over the importance that should be attached to this mode, stringent regulations that vary from one country to another, a lack of standardization between networks, a fragmented sector and segregated markets. This is the reason for the lack of forceful measures and the hesitant approach. While France remained inert, Germany responded vigorously with the Leber Plan and the Act of 8 January 1969, which paved the way for the emergence of co-operatives 25 years before they appeared in France. Except for a few measures, such as the navigability certificate in 1976 and the consultation procedure for transport infrastructure projects, there was still no coherent European transport policy in 1981. Under pressure from the European Parliament, some twenty or so individual measures were subsequently taken with regard to waterway transport. The Judgement of the Court of Justice of the EC in May 1985, following the Single Act, provided fresh impetus and a new market began to take shape. However, in order to liberalise the market, the fleet first needed to be restructured, and this was provided by the "scrap and build" mechanism and the first scrapping schemes. The EEC acted in place of governments with Directive No. 1101/89. The Maastricht Treaty, ratified in 1992, made provision for the creation of European networks. The "scrap and build" mechanism was maintained, although did not prove to be wholly satisfactory. As a result, Regulation 3690/92 was introduced to strengthen the mechanism and to redefine the notion of active fleet. At the same time, Regulation No. 3921/91 and the Ruling of 16 December 1993 set out the conditions applicable to cabotage. This was the first step towards creation of a single market in all Community Member States on 1 January 1995. The internal regulations of Member States had to be reviewed from a more liberal standpoint and the practice of chartering by rotation was challenged. On 1 January 1994, Germany abolished mandatory tariffs. The key objectives now were to liberalise, restructure and promote the waterways. France set an example with the Act of July 1994 on commercial organisation. The EU gave priority to co-operation between carriers, which led to the emergence of co-operatives -- a long-standing practice in the Netherlands and Germany -- in France. In addition, governments were encouraged to intervene by assuming responsibility for problems relating to inland navigation. This led to co-operation between authorities, culminating in the creation of the European Federation of Inland Ports on 20 April 1994 in Brussels. Following the collapse of communism, the EU was too slow to open up to the East and only began to do so once the Rhine-Main-Danube link had already been opened. At this point, the EU came into conflict with the CCR which, through the additional protocol to the Act of Mannheim, had restricted access by East European fleets to the Rhine market. Germany and the Netherlands signed bilateral agreements with the CEECs, condemned by the EU in 1996. The EU, with support from Belgium, France and Switzerland and in collaboration with the CCR, subsequently negotiated multilateral agreements with the CEECs that rendered all other bilateral agreements null and void. The problem of networks then arose. The start of an infrastructure policy dates back to the Regulation of 20 November 1990 which was designed to set out a programme of action with regard to transport infrastructure and which made it possible, under certain conditions, for infrastructure projects to qualify for Community funding. Title XII of the Treaty on European Union, signed in Maastricht, considers transport infrastructure from the standpoint of trans-European networks. Without waiting for the Treaty to be ratified, the Commission began work on drawing up plans for the projected network. As part of this planning work, the Commission submitted a communication to both the Council and the Parliament on issues relating to trans-European transport networks, a proposed amendment to Regulation 3359/90, a report of the actions in progress and three proposed network plans (combined rail transport and combined waterway transport). The forecast growth in traffic flows in Europe justified the urgency of this policy, the use of inland waterways and the promotion of intermodality. The interconnection and interoperability of existing national networks were fundamental objectives. With regard to the drafting of the Trans-European Network Outline Plan (see map), the unofficial Council of Ministers' meeting in Rotterdam on 5 and 6 July 1990 proved to be a turning point, with a decision to give priority to two major corridors: the North-South corridor (Escaut-Seine link, Seine-Moselle, Seine-Saône) and the East-West corridor (Rotterdam, Antwerp, Berlin and Poland), thus establishing a waterway network for combined transport operations. These Outline Plans were endorsed by the Council of Ministers on 29 October 1993. To meet its concerns over damage to the environment and external costs, the EU drew up a Green Book in 1996. Following on directly from this initiative, the Commission proposed to the Council of Ministers that the PACT programme (Pilot Action for Combined Transport) be extended to 2001 and be allocated further funding of Ecu 35 million. The EU then pursued its work on harmonization by asking the Council of Ministers to adopt a Directive on the harmonization of the conditions for obtaining national boatmasters' certificates for navigation on inland waterways (Directive published in the OJ of 1 September 1996). However, the

EU does not have the necessary resources to implement the projects approved at the Essen Summit. All that it can do is to encourage the private sector to act in its place. If the EU wishes to make its presence felt with regard to eastern Europe, it will once again find itself facing major funding requirements. It also seems unable to take any type of measure to initiate the internalisation of external costs. The issue of taxation is also unresolved. Given these problems, it would seem that implementation of the Outline Plan has got off to a bad start; the only parts of it that may be put in place will probably be those which governments are prepared to undertake, failing a reform of the way in which the Union works. The development strategies recommended by the UN/ECE or the ECMT have also run into the same problems.

The international commissions for navigation on the Rhine, the Moselle and the Danube

By harmonizing their strategies and the role they play in their respective river basins, the commissions are, in most cases, encouraging development of the inland waterways market. At present, there are not enough dry docks on the Rhine.

Port authorities and network managers

- The maritime ports must enhance the quality of the sea/inland waterway interface by eliminating the various discriminatory practices that apply to this mode. This effort will only prove fruitful if it is pursued in collaboration with operators.
  The Barge Control Centre, set up in response to an initiative of the *Fahrgemeinschaft Niederrhein* in Rotterdam, was set up to improve the co-ordination of the activities of operators, vessels and port terminals. It allows operators to reduce the waiting times for container barges and thus lower costs. The operators from the various pools can thereby strengthen their negotiating position with regard to stevedores. The barge control centre, which functions 24 hours a day, is open to all actors in the transport chain. The system is computer-based and makes use of ultra-sophisticated communications systems;
- River ports, by providing technical assistance and by acting as prime contractor for any work needed on the waterfront, can encourage charterers to ship their goods by waterway (e.g. the Paris port authority). The system of farming out contracts might help to promote this mode. Some ports, by virtue of their location, may be able to promote themselves as advance ports. These inland ports have a

considerable potential as logistical operators upon which to capitalise. Their future lies in their multi-functionality.

Co-operation between ports in border areas is a necessity. It would allow investments to be made on a rational basis and would also afford major economies of scale. The co-operation between France, Germany and Switzerland in the Basel region (Basel-Weil-Rhine ports of southern Alsace) improves the management of North-South flows and ensures that infrastructure is more competitive. Collaboration between the ports of Strasbourg and Kiel has proved to be highly rewarding. The same would be true for many ports on the Danube, for example, between Bulgarian and Romanian ports such as Kladovo and Turnu-Severin, Vidin and Calafat, Bechet and Orjahovo, Turnu-Magurele and Nikopol, Zimnicea and Svistov, Giurgiu and Ruse, Tutrakan and Oltenita, Calarasi, Ostrov and Silistra.

There should be more alliances of the *Aproport* type in port management (French port entity, grouping together the ports of Villefranche, Mâcon, Chalon sur Saône, with the aim of providing improved management and productivity). To ensure their success, they must be highly flexible;

− Network managers must encourage the creation of waterway connections at competitive prices, the construction of multimodal platforms with quayside frontage, the elimination of discriminatory tariffs through an astute marketing policy and renewed interest from charterers;

− By joining forces, waterway operators, whether vessel owners or charterers, can add to their logistical supply and ensure a better match between their carrying capacity and demand without necessarily having to subjugate themselves to the pressures of maritime charterers;

− Competition with the rail sector must give way to complementarity. The growth in combined transport and the creation of freeways might seem to be a worst-case scenario. Would the emergence of rail operators owned by the maritime sector be any more reassuring? These operators also use the inland waterways!

4.2. What are tomorrow's markets?

The choice of energy source, whether it be nuclear, coal or hydrogen, will be determining for the future:

– Could coal be a viable energy source for the 21st ce
substantial reserves of coal and, as an energy source,
readily available, relatively secure from a politic
found in abundance throughout the world. Total
amounts to 3.6 billion tonnes a year. Coal is be
Europe, however, particularly in western Europe,
Kingdom produces 53 million tonnes, Germany
Spain 18 million tonnes and France 7 million tonnes a year. Mines in
these countries are now starting to close. There are only two major
coal-producing countries in central and eastern Europe: the Czech
Republic, which produces some 18 million tonnes a year and Poland
which produces 132 million tonnes. Imports to Europe should
therefore rise rapidly. In addition to European flows originating in
Poland, which exported 32 million tonnes of coal in 1995, there are
also rising flows of coal from overseas areas such as North America,
Australia, South Africa and even Asia. Imports to western Europe are
the second highest in the world and grew 7 per cent to 131 million
tonnes: Italy, 19 million tonnes; the Netherlands, 18 million tonnes;
the United Kingdom, 16 million tonnes; France, 14 million tonnes;
Germany, 17 million tonnes; Spain, 13 million tonnes. Imports to
eastern Europe amounted to 22 million tonnes. Imports to western
Europe are set to increase still further as the European mining industry
continues to decline.

Electricity in most countries is still largely generated in fossil-fired
plants: the Netherlands, 94 per cent; Germany, 67 per cent; Belgium,
40 per cent; Austria, 32 per cent; Bulgaria, 50 per cent; Hungary,
59 per cent; Romania, 80 per cent; the Czech Republic, 61 per cent.
The nuclear power plants in eastern European countries pose a number
of problems. There is also the question of the choice that France will
make once it has to replace its current installed nuclear capacity.
Despite the use of oil in the United States, coal accounts for 40 per
cent of electricity production. World reserves of coal are extremely
large and amount to six times the world's oil reserves and three times
its reserves of gas. Europe's energy requirements will increase,
particularly in eastern Europe;

– Ore and scrap flows will inevitably stabilize. However, the technical
efficiency of the steel and specialty steel industries in Europe should help
to maintain these activities, which will generate flows in steel products;

– Fertilisers, which may increasingly be supplied by eastern European
countries;

– The level of oil products should remain stable, since the pipeline
network does not cover the whole of Europe;

149

The chemical industry is making increasing use of the inland waterways for transport;

- Construction materials as a result of the major infrastructure and reconstruction programmes in central and eastern Europe, particularly in view of the fact that, under current legislation, firms are no longer allowed to extract sand and gravel from the bed or the edge of the minor beds of rivers;
- The future of agro-food flows remains uncertain. The EU's desire to reduce cereal exports from the Communities in order to recapture the internal market, particularly the animal feed market, may lead to a decline in the volume of products transported by waterway. It is possible, however, that this policy might prompt animal feed industries to move to sites located on waterways and to transport their finished products to major animal-rearing regions through chains incorporating waterway or waterway/maritime legs. European cereal production should nonetheless remain stable and should continue to generate export flows of comparable volume to present flows.
Efforts to create jobs are leading us to give added value to agricultural products in various forms that are capable of generating flows of goods with high added value;
- Machinery, manufactured goods and vehicles should generate large flows of both containerised and non-containerised goods;
- Containerised traffic flows, adapted to all types of goods, will enjoy spectacular growth in all networks;
- Specialised transport flows are certain to grow; growth in this area in France in 1996 amounted to over 15 per cent;
- There is scope for substantial growth in traffic flows of all types of goods in the maritime ports;
- The new flows generated by the deployment of new waterway transport technologies and the use of waterway/maritime transport will continue to grow. There will be dramatic growth in the latter;
- Combined waterway transport will continue to grow;
- The transport of household and industrial wastes are promising markets.

Tourism is also a growing source of demand for network use and, in this respect, there is much ground to be made up. The two types of usage must be mutually acceptable, even on major arteries.

Table 19. Cost of transport between Rotterdam-Central Europe (DM/t)

Origin/ Destination	Road	Rail	Inland waterway
Vienna	110.62	124.77	64.47
Bratislava	110.62	126.54	69.01
Budapest	123.90	134.50	72.56
Belgrade	188.50	151.31	77.87

This cannot happen unless there is a clear resolve on the part of international organisations, the EU and governments to promote the use of the inland waterways. It should be noted that the inland waterways is the mode which best covers overall costs (both internal and external) while still being capable of providing just-in-time deliveries, and which will remain the cheapest form of transport in the future, even though the cost of rail freight can be expected to fall with the entry of new operators into the market. In the United States, open access to the network of private operators (Stagger Act) stimulates supply and has allowed combined transport to grow substantially.

The development of the waterways will therefore require growth in combined rail/waterway transport systems in the inland ports (Duisburg, Basel, Linz, Vienna, Bratislava, Vidin, Dresden, Liège, Lille, Lyons, etc.).

In this particular configuration, the Mediterranean ports (Algeçiras, Barcelona, Marseilles or Sète, Genoa, Venice, Trieste, Cagliari-Tauro) will serve not only the Mediterranean Basin, but also the states of the former Yugoslavia, through combined rail or waterway/maritime transport chains. Marsaxlokk will play the same role by means of feeders. In South-East Europe, Thessalonika or Cyprus will provide the same services.

This development will therefore be accompanied by strong growth in the waterway/maritime sector of 10-20 per cent a year and more. Europe has much ground to catch up in this area compared with the United States and Japan, which use the waterways to transport over a billion tonnes of goods a year. The waterways are the most efficient mode of transport provided that current tariff distortions can be eradicated.

As a result, growth in road transport should level off.

The trend towards mega-vessels continues. The enlarged Europe now encompasses all European states except for Russia, Ukraine and Belarus. The rate of economic growth is still modest (2 to 2.5 per cent a year) in western European countries, but at 9 per cent is much higher in CEECs. After initial recovery, these countries are now starting to catch up. The economies of North-East and South-East Asia continue to grow at a rate of 4-5 per cent a year, growth in Latin America is accelerating (7-8 per cent), growth in Africa has risen to 3-4 per cent, driven by growth in South Africa and possibly Egypt.

European output is increasingly specialised in high-technology and its energy needs are being met by large, coal-fired power plants. The development of nuclear fusion power would completely change the situation. Most of the planned inland waterways have been completed.

1st scenario: The rise of the Baltic ports as well as those in the Aegean and the Black Sea

The ports of North-West Europe (Rotterdam, Hamburg, Antwerp, Zeebrugge, Le Havre?) are still major players, but there is growth in containerised traffic from the ports of Swinoujscie and Gdynia on the Baltic Sea. Traffic is growing on the North-South corridor along the Oder-Danube waterway, and also on the East-West corridor, particularly now that the Vistula-Bug link has been completed. There is also growth in combined rail transport. Waterway traffic towards the Baltic States and Russia is increasing. This strategy was foreseen as far back as 1996 by the Port of Rotterdam, which is now trying to enter into more partnerships with the Baltic State ports (Riga, Tallin, etc.), while Hamburg is setting up waterway/maritime services to Moscow along the Neva. The Russian market and that of part of the CIS have therefore become strategic targets for Poland, Germany and the Netherlands.

Meanwhile, the volume of traffic continues to grow on the Rhine, particularly on the upper and middle reaches. Traffic on the Rhine-Main-Danube Canal is also continuing to grow and similarly that on the Danube, which now underpins the organisation of the entire economy of the Danube region. Traffic on this river now amounts to over 150-200 million tonnes. Regional integration is now well advanced.

In southern Europe, Thessalonika, Sulina, Constanta and Odessa are starting to emerge as major ports, feeding waterway/maritime traffic to the ports on the Danube and merchant ports on the shores of the European states on the Black Sea. These ports also generate major flows of combined rail transport.

This scenario therefore sees a balance restored in surface flows, together with ever closer regional integration.

2nd scenario: *No major development of the Baltic ports or those on the Aegean or Black Sea coast*

The major port organisations of North-West Europe are growing stronger. Despite growth in French ports as a result of the opening of the Seine-North and Rhine-Rhône links, the surface transport networks are no longer capable of functioning properly. The traditional North-South and East-West corridors are overloaded. Transport is the main cause of environmental damage. European traffic flows will probably amount to over 30-40 billion tonnes, if not more. The situation will be all the more critical if the share of waterway/maritime remains modest and the share of the waterways remains stable at 6 per cent. To avoid such congestion, the German proposals would seem to be the most sensible ones. There must be an annual increase of 15-20 per cent in the volume of long-haul freight shipped by waterway. The ideal modal split would be 30/30/30. This model would certainly be feasible provided that maritime vessels use the inland waterways. It would clearly be unrealistic to attempt to achieve this objective without activistic policies. Zero growth will perhaps prevent us from addressing such problems.

CONCLUSION

The inland waterway transport sector is currently undergoing a period of change. Traditionally reserved for the transport of bulk and dry goods, of which tonnages are now declining, the inland waterways are now turning to new markets and are starting to take an interest in high value-added and containerised freight.

To do this, the waterways have been incorporated into the most modern logistical chains and have proved to be highly flexible. Inland waterways can readily be used for just-in-place and just-in-time deliveries. They can also be used by both industry and major distributors alike.

The waterways are the ideal partner for major maritime ports. With the trend towards mega-vessels, these two modes are becoming increasingly interrelated, particularly in view of the scope for new development afforded by the combination of inland waterways and ocean-going shipping. At present, the

European Main Ports are also the major river ports in Europe. The control that maritime shippers are now acquiring over inland transport cannot but accelerate this process.

This renaissance is also linked to that of the inland ports, which are developing into logistical operators. All these ports have invested in modern infrastructure and are all multimodal platforms. The more dynamic among them are developing into up-river ports.

The composition of vessel fleets is constantly being adapted by both charterers and owner-operators in order to supply the market with high-capacity vessels that offer a high degree of flexibility in terms of both transport and loading/unloading operations. Scrapping is therefore no longer on the agenda for fleets operating on certain arteries such as the Rhine and the Rhône.

Inland waterways offer the highest cost-effectiveness for both short-haul shipments and long-haul international transport. In both geographical and economic terms, inland waterways seem to be perfectly suited for operations at a European level. However, cultural factors and image are the determining factors in whether or not this mode will be promoted by governments. Genuine progress in the use of this mode will need an activistic policy on the part of governments, the EU and international institutions.

Why have the inland waterways declined to such an extent? Although attributable in part to trends in the economy, this decline is the outcome of the fierce competition between road and rail transport and also the neglect into which some governments have allowed the inland waterways to fall by fencing the sector in with excessively detailed regulations, such as the chartering by rotation system which prevented charterers from choosing which carrier to use! Lack of maintenance and a failure to upgrade infrastructure simply added impetus to the decline. This mode is not an election-winner, particularly in countries that are only now beginning to discover environmental issues.

However, unless efforts to modernise infrastructure actually start to materialise, the inland waterways cannot expect to develop a large and up-to-date market. The inland waterways must not become the forgotten mode of transport policy. They are the main alternative mode to choose if we wish to protect our environment.

NOTES

1. Studies carried out by Planco Consulting Gmbh and published by Binnenschiffahrt; study carried out by the Transport Circle of the Ministerial Working Party on CO_2 Reduction in October 1990, Ministry of Transport, Bonn.

2. Infrastructure and external social costs.

ANNEXES

ANNEX 1

Number of vessels by country

	Austria	Belgium	France	Germany	Netherlands	Switzerland
1975	203	4 182	6 563	4 786	8 146	423
1980	194	3 001	5 224	3 812	6 535	394
1985	213	2 513	4 729	3 143	6 371	335
1990	120	1 778	3 068	2 723	6 282	169
1991	204	1 639	2 813	1 574	6 011	151
1992					5 681	144
1993					5 524	

Number of vessels

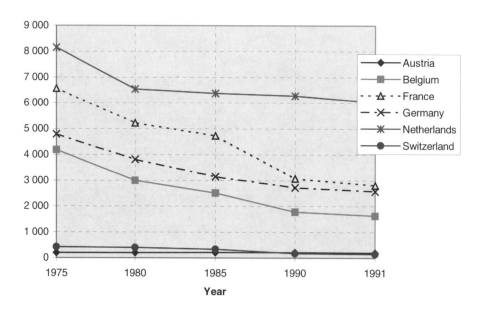

160

Average carrying capacity of vessels

	Austria	Belgium	France	Germany	Netherlands	Switzerland
1975	1 029	555	447	882	628	1 359
1980	1 009	615	486	963	750	1 503
1985	1 116	688	488	1 043	855	1 730
1990	1 228	857	539	1 122	973	1 902
1991	1 232	894	546	1 148	997	1 923
1992					1 028	1 956
1993					1 058	

Trends in average carrying capacity of vessels

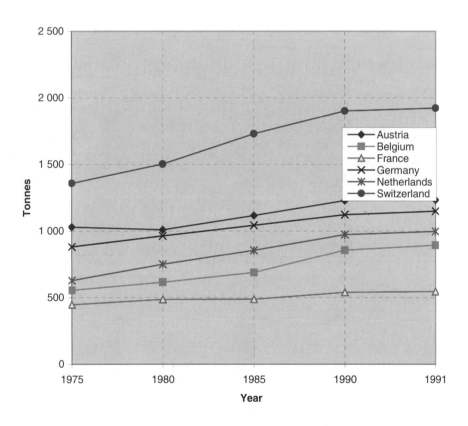

Total carrying capacity of national inland waterway fleets

	Austria	Belgium	France	Germany	Netherlands	Switzerland
1975	208 850	2 321 000	2 940 000	4 221 812	5 117 000	575 000
1980	195 790	1 844 000	2 537 052	3 671 963	4 900 000	592 000
1985	237 711	1 729 412	2 308 044	3 276 622	5 477 000	579 685
1990	257 924	1 523 301	1 652 600	3 055 923	6 113 000	321 508
1991	251 414	1 465 099	1 535 420	2 955 517	5 994 000	290 341
1992					5 840 000	281 719
1993					5 842 000	

Total carrying capacity of national inland waterway fleets

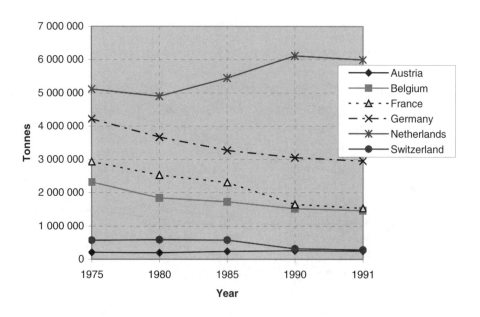

ANNEX 2

Operators in 1996

Inland waterway operators in the Netherlands

CTG Rotterdam	Scheduled services between Rotterdam and Germersheim.
Danser Container Line	Operator on the Rhine and Danube canals. Services between Rotterdam, Amsterdam, Strasbourg, Ottmarsheim, Basel. Connections with Rhine Container and Interrijn to Germany and Austria. Door-to-door deliveries available.
Danube Container Service	Joint venture between Interrijn, Rhine Container and Penta Container Line. Door-to-door services available.
Dubbelman Container Transport	Scheduled services between the Netherlands, Belgium, France, Germany and Switzerland.
Eurobarge	Daily service between Rotterdam and Antwerp.
Haniel Reederei	Service from Benelux ports to the lower, middle and upper Rhine. Door-to-door service available.
Interrijn	Operates on the Danube Container line in conjunction with Rhine Container and Penta Container Line, and the Rhine RoRo Service with RSG Rhenania and Nedlloyd Rijn-en Binnenvaart.
MTA Freight Service	Service between Rotterdam and Antwerp.
Penta Container Line	Operates on the Danube Container Line with Rhine container and Interrijn.
Rhine Container	Operates services on the Rhine between the Netherlands and Germany. Also an operator on the Danube Container Service together with Interrijn and Penta Container Line.
Rhine RoRo Service	Joint Venture between Interrijn, Nedlloyd Rijn en Binnenvaart and RSG Rhenania.
RSG Rhenania	Operates on the Rhine RoRo Service in conjunction with Interrijn and Nedlloyd Rijn-en Binnenvaart.

Inland waterway operators in Switzerland

Penta Container line	Transport services on the Rhine between Antwerp, Rotterdam and Basel.
SILAG (St-Johan Lagerhaus & Schiffahrts Gesellschaft)	Transport on the Rhine from Benelux ports towards Basel in association with auxiliary companies SILAG Natural Van Dam and SPEDAG Rheinschiffahrts AG. Door-to-door delivery available.
SRN Schwerische Reederei und Neptune	Transport between its own terminals and the entire European river network.

Inland waterway operators in Austria

Combined Container Service (CCS)	Dutch company serving 15 destinations on the Rhine, the Main and the Danube (Vienna, Krems, Linz, etc.)
Danube Container Service	Service between the Netherlands, Germany, Austria, Hungary and the Slovak Republic;
Wasserkombi	Operates between Austria and Antwerp, Rotterdam, Amsterdam, Budapest. Rail link in Vienna towards eastern Europe.

Inland waterway operators in Belgium

Dubbelman Container Transporten	Dutch company operating services to France, Belgium and Switzerland.
Contship Containerlines NV Containerships Antwerp Maats Intermodal System Tracto NV Avelgem Cont. Terminal NV	
CFNR	From France to the Netherlands, Belgium and Switzerland.
CEM	Service between Antwerp and Rotterdam, Zeebrugge
FINNBELGIA SRN Alpina (Surzerbas) Tor Line NV	
NWL	Norddeutsche Wasserweg Logistik

Inland waterway operators in Bulgaria

Navigation Marit. Bulgare

National company operating in the Black Sea, northern Europe and the Mediterranean.

Unimasters Logistics Group

Inland waterway operators in the Czech Republic

LABE Container Line

Operates on the Elbe.

Inland waterway operators in France

Compagnie Française de Navigation Rhénane

Operates on the Rhine and the Danube.

Delta Box

Operates between Marseilles, Fos, Lyons, Macon and Châlon.

ALCOTRANS

Operates on the Rhine in France, offering services to the Netherlands, Germany and Switzerland.

Inland waterway operators in Germany

Combined Container Service (CCS)

Contship Containerlines

Deutsche Binnenreederei

Operates 54-TEU barges on the Elbe between Hamburg and Prague.

SRN Alpina

Frankenbach Container Service

Operates on the Rhine between Rotterdam, Mayenz, Hoechst and Wirth.

Gernsheimer Umschlags und Terminalbetrie (GUT)

Operates services between Benelux countries and middle Rhine.

Haniel Reederei

Operates services on the Rhine from Benelux countries.

KSW Systems

Haeger und Schmidt

Operates services from Antwerp and Rotterdam to the Rhine ports. Also operates services on other inland/maritime waterways.

Norddeutsche Wasserweg Logistik
(NWL).
Operates primarily on inland/maritime waterways.

Inland waterway operators in Hungary

Mahart Hungarian
Shipping Company
Operates services from the Danube ports to the Black Sea.
Inland/maritime services to the continent.

	Distance from Rotterdam in km	Capacity in TEU/year
NETHERLANDS		
DEN BOSCH	85	
BORN	200	30 000
COEVORDEN	250	3 000
MEPPEL	190	20 000
NIJMEGEN	120	45 000
OSS	100	50 000
AUSTRIA		
KREMS/DONAU	1 200	60 000
VIENNA	1 150	150 000
LINZ		
BELGIUM		
AVELGEM		
CZECH REPUBLIC		
MELNIK		12 000
FRANCE		
STRASBOURG	700	65 000
OTTMARSHEIM	800	50 966
GERMANY		
BERLIN	800	150 000
BONN	300	50 000
DORTMUND	230	150 000
DUISBURG	150	150 000
EMMERICH		
GEMERSHEIM	635	250 000
GERNSHEIM		40 000
KEHL AM RHEIN	700	30 000
KIEL	600	20 000
COLOGNE	300	70 000
LUDWIGSHAFEN	550	50 000
NEU ULM	800	
RAVENSBURG		10 000
STUTTGART	500	10 000
WEIL AM RHEIN	830	10 000
HUNGARY		
BUDAPEST		
SLOVAKIA		
BRATISLAVA	1 350	20 000

Containerised goods entering and leaving the Port of Rotterdam (million tonnes)

Year	1988	1989	1990	1991	1992	1993*	1994*
Entering							
Imports	15.2	14.4	17.2	17.1	19.8	24.3	23.1
stored in warehouse	2.0	2.0	0.5	0.6	0.6	1.0	1.9
goods in transit	0.5	0.2	0.5	0.6	0.6	1.0	1.9
	12.7	12.2	14.5	14.4	15.9	18.9	18.4
Leaving							
Export	17.3	16.5	19.0	19.1	20.5	22.1	21.5
taken from storage	4.5	4.1	4.2	4.3	4.4	3.1	2.6
in transit	0	0	0.3	0.2	0.1	0.1	0.3
	12.8	12.3	14.6	14.5	16.0	18.9	18.6

Excluding goods in transit within Europe.
Source: Statistics Nederlands, Heerlen.

**Containerised goods entering and leaving the Port of Rotterdam
by type of good in 1994 (million tonnes)**

	Entering	Leaving
TOTAL	23 058	21 526
Agricultural produce and livestock	1 793	1 574
Food products	3 926	4 420
Solid mineral fuels	390	43
Oil products	150	134
Metal ores and scrap	245	313
Metals and semi-finished metals	1 552	1 570
Unprocessed ores, building materials	644	555
Fertilisers	83	82
Chemical products	5 433	5 384
Other merchandise and products	8 841	7 450

Excluding goods in transit within Europe.
According to NSTR chapter on goods.

**Containerised goods entering and leaving the port of Rotterdam
by mode of transport in 1994 (million tonnes)**

	Total	Imported	Warehoused	Transit
Entering				
Barge	2 048	41	6	2 001
Rail	734	4	8	722
Road	6 558	77	6	6 474
Leaving				
Barge	2 056	6	5	2 045
Rail	797	2	15	780
Road	1 876	55	46	1 775

FORECAST GROWTH IN THE
CONTAINER HANDLING CAPACITY OF PORTS

Port/Terminal

Le Havre

Pacific Basin II	1997	300
	1998	500

Port 2000

Antwerp

Scheldt II	1997	300
	1998	350
Scheldt III	2005	350

Zeebrugge

FCT II	1995	500
Hessenatie	1997	600
FCT III	1999	250

Rotterdam

2008 II	1996	500
2008 III	1999	500
2008 IV	2000	500
2008 V/VI	2005	1 000

Bremerhaven

CT III	1998	500

Hamburg

Burchardkai	1996	150
Tollerort	1997	150
	1998	150
Eurokai	1996	150
	1997	150
Altenwerder	2002	500
	2004	500

Total by around 2005		7 900

BIBLIOGRAPHY

(1995), *Un marché, BULGARIE*, Poste d'expansion économique à Sofia, Les Editions du CFCE, February, ISBN 2-279-41031-1, 151 pp.

(1995), *Un marché, HONGRIE*, Poste d'expansion économique à Budapest, Les Editions du CFCE, March, ISBN 2-279-41013-3, 208 pp.

(1996), *Un marché, ROUMANIE*, Poste d'expansion économique à Bucarest, Les Editions du CFCE, May, ISBN 2-279-41041-9, 158 pp.

(1996), *Un marché, SLOVAQUIE*, Poste d'expansion économique à Bratislava, Les Editions du CFCE, December, ISBN 2-279-41123-7, 158 pp.

Agence Française de l'Ingénierie Touristique (1995), *Le tourisme fluvial en France*, Ministère du Tourisme, 101pp.

Blanc, A., P. George, H. Smotkine, *Les Républiques Socialistes d'Europe centrale,* Presses Universitaires de France, coll. Magellan No. 15, 298 pp.

Chatelus, G. (1993), *Les transports en Europe centrale -- Inadéquation de l'offre face à une demande restructurée*, INRETS-OEST, Paradigme, November, ISBN 2-86878-113-6, 187 pp.

Chavigny, B. (1996), *Spécialisation internationale et transition en Europe centrale et Orientale*, L'Harmattan, coll. "Pays de l'Est", January, ISBN 2-7384-4002-9, 255 pp.

Conseil Economique et Social (1993), "Les ports maritimes et fluviaux, leur place dans l'économie française et leur rôle dans l'aménagement du territoire", report submitted by Mr. Jacques Brunier, Direction des journaux officiels, 178 pp.

Damien, M.M. (1997), *Les Transports Fluviaux,* Presses Universitaires de France, coll. Que sais-je?, March, 128 pp.

Damien, M.M. (1995), "Situation, problèmes et prospectives d'évolution de la navigation fluviale dans l'Europe du Marché Commun", Doctoral thesis, Université de Nantes, 9 January, 1 228 pp.

Delobez, A., *et al.* (1996), *Images économiques du monde 1996-1997*, SEDES, October, ISBN 2-7181-9014-0, 416 pp., as well as earlier volumes in the same collection.

Drevet, J.F. (1991), *La France et l'Europe des régions*, Paris, SYROS-Alternatives, 235 pp.

Dron, D. (1995), *Pour une politique soutenable des transports*, Documentation Française, coll. rapports officiels, Paris, September.

ECMT (1995), *Transport Infrastructure in Central and Eastern European Countries. Selection Criteria and Funding*, ISBN 92-821-2203-4, 145 pp.

ECMT (1995), *Transport: New Problems, New Solutions*, 13th Symposium, Luxembourg, 9-11 May, ISBN 92-821-2212-3, 724 pp.

Gaspard, M. (1996), *Le financement des infrastructures de transport en Europe centrale et Orientale - Evolutions et Perspectives*, Presses de l'Ecole Nationale des Ponts et Chaussées, November, ISBN 2-85978-268-0, 141 pp.

Institut Planco Consulting Gmbh (1990*), External costs of rail, road and inland waterway traffic,* Bonn, October, published by Binnenschiffahrt, study carried out by the Transport Circle of the Ministerial Working Party on CO_2 Reduction.

IWW and INFRAS (1994), *Effets externes du transport*, Karlsruhe, Zurich, November.

Lhomel, E. (1995), *Transitions économiques à l'Est (1989-1995)*, CEDUCEE, Les études de la Documentation Française, December, ISBN 2-11-003465-3, 262 pp.

Revue Navigation Ports et Industrie, Editions de la Navigation du Rhin, Strasbourg.

United Nations Economic Commission for Europe (1996), *White Paper on trends in and development of inland navigation*, TRANS/SC.3/138, Geneva.

United Nations Economic Commission for Europe (1996), *Economic Bulletin for Europe*, Volume 48, New York and Geneva, ISBN 92-1-116660-8, 145 pp.

Voies Navigables de France (1995), *Statistique annuelle de la navigation intérieure -- 1995*, Ministère de l'Equipement, du Transport et du Tourisme, 239 pp.

NETHERLANDS

Pieter HILFERINK
Director of Research
NEA
Rijswijk
Netherlands

ACKNOWLEDGEMENTS

This contribution is chiefly based on the following studies:

- *Towards a European Policy for the Inland Waterway Industry*, NEA/Planco, 1991;

- *Analysis of Traffic Flows Within the Framework of the Trans-European Inland Waterways Network*, NEA/Planco, 1994;

- *Medium/Longterm Forecasts of the Modal Share in Goods Transport Demand*, NEA, 1994;

- *Containers Barge Ahead*, NEA, 1995.

Through this approach, the present contribution includes studies carried out by Philippe Tardieu and Marinus van den Elshout, who have made suggestions for and comments on this report.

SUMMARY

Rijswijk, February 1997

1. THE HISTORICAL DEVELOPMENT OF
INLAND WATERWAY TRANSPORT

The history of inland waterway transport (IWT) goes back several centuries. Though interesting in itself, in this context a description of its history is not relevant for its future market position. The first competitors for inland shipping were railway companies. Railways were faster but more expensive so, in cases where appropriate waterway infrastructure was available and where price was an important element in the choice of mode, the railways could not win this competition. Later on, road transport became the most important mode, taking over the major part of short-distance transport and a considerable part of interregional transport. This development continued well into the seventies and eighties.

The development from 1975 to 1988 in the western European market is shown in Tables 1 and 2 below.

Table 1. **Total volumes in IWT in the Netherlands, West Germany, Belgium, Luxembourg and France -- 1975 and 1988 (million tonnes)**

	1975	**1988**	**Index 1975-88**
Domestic	230	204	89
International	189	221	117
Total	419	426	101

Source: Towards a European Policy for the Inland Waterway Industry,
    NEA/Planco, 1991.

Table 2. Index of volumes (tonnes) of IWT in selected markets (index 1975-88)

	Domestic	Export	Import	Total
West Germany	80	107	118	99
Netherlands	116	121	112	115
Belgium	103	141	133	121
France	56	87	98	64

Source: Towards a European Policy for the Inland Waterway Industry,
           NEA/Planco, 1991.

During this period, the main IWT corridors in Europe were the Rhine (growing by 15 per cent between 1975 and 1988), the North-South axis (with more or less constant volumes) and the East-West axis (down by 15 per cent between 1970 and 1988).

1.1. West Germany

Domestic transport on inland waterways in the Federal Republic of Germany decreased from 1975 to 1988 by 20 per cent, whereas international transport increased by 14 per cent. Exports grew from 49.5 million tonnes to 53.0 million tonnes. In particular, transport to Belgium increased significantly. Transport to the Netherlands decreased during this period but, with 55.6 per cent of total exports, still represented the most important portion, its bulk consisting predominantly of crude or processed mineral products, building materials and chemical products.

As regards exports to Belgium, metal products played a major role (24.1 per cent) besides building materials (24.3 per cent), chemical products (10.5 per cent) and fertiliser (11.6 per cent).

Imports increased during the same period from 85.6 million tonnes to 100.7 million tonnes. Seventy-five per cent of all imports resulted from or were imported via the Netherlands.

1.2. The Netherlands

In the Netherlands, domestic waterway transport was able to expand by 16 per cent between 1975 and 1988. International transport increased by 18 per cent from 135.9 million tonnes to 161.1 million tonnes.

Exports by IWT developed from 92.0 million tonnes to 111.8 million tonnes. In 1988, 66 per cent of exports transported by the inland waterway transport industry went to Germany, consisting mainly of iron ores (48.2 per cent) and oil products (23.5 per cent). Furthermore, transport to Belgium played a significant role, 26.8 per cent of total exports. Main commodity groups were crude or processed mineral products, building materials and oil products. Imports predominantly originated from Germany (60 per cent) and Belgium (30 per cent), although transport from France expanded significantly.

1.3. Belgium

Domestic waterway transport increased slightly from 21.5 to 22.1 million tonnes. The strong increase in the Belgian waterway transport market resulted mainly from the expansion of international transport, which grew from 54.8 to 74.5 million tonnes.

Of the related exports, 41.8 per cent were directed to the Netherlands, concentrating on commodities such as building materials and oil products but also including a considerable share of machines, vehicles and manufactured goods (9.8 per cent).

Exports to Germany consisted mainly of oil products and chemical products, both commodities together accounting for 49.4 per cent of these exports. Also noteworthy are metal products (9.7 per cent), building materials (8.5 per cent) and fertiliser (8.4 per cent).

The most significant imports came from Germany and the Netherlands with, among them, 90 per cent of all imports via inland waterways. They increased considerably, by 39 per cent and 44 per cent respectively, during the period between 1975 and 1988.

1.4. France

Domestic waterway transport in France decreased dramatically (by 44 per cent) and international transport slightly (by 9 per cent). The dominant partner concerning exports via inland waterway is Germany. These exports mainly consist of building materials, food products and oil products. Whereas transport to Belgium also decreased, transport to the Netherlands expanded by 43 per cent. Main commodities are agricultural products, building materials and solid mineral fuels. Importation via waterways remained relatively stable, the main importing countries being Germany, the Netherlands and Belgium.

1.5. ECMT statistics

The ECMT has published developments in tonne-kms for all its Member countries (see Table 3).

Table 3. **Percentage modal split share (tonne-kms) of the different modes in ECMT countries**

	1970	1975	1980	1985	1990	1994
Railways	31	25	23	21	17	16
Road	55	63	66	69	74	76
Inland waterway	14	12	11	10	9	8

Source: ECMT.

In 1994, the total number of tonne-kms transported in the ECMT countries rose from 857 billion in 1970 to 1.528 billion. Inland waterway transport has been more or less constant in this period (about 110 billion tonne-kms), thus leading to a lower market share.

From all the inland waterway tonne-kms in the total ECMT area, the share in volumes in the two major countries, Germany and the Netherlands, has risen from 75 per cent in 1970 to over 80 per cent in 1994. Together with Belgium and France, this share was almost 95 per cent in 1994. From the remaining 5 per cent, more than half was realised in Finland.

The developments in market share in the period 1970 to 1994 show the following trends:

–   Relative decline of the volumes in those types of goods where inland waterway is strong;
–   Loss of a large part of the market in general cargo to road transport;
–   A stronger position compared to railways in the type of goods, relations and distance classes where rail and inland waterway are the main competitors.

In the Central and Eastern European Countries (the ten PECO countries), developments have been different. Here, the total market for land transport grew until 1988, then fell below the level of 1970. The share of inland waterway declined from 3 per cent in 1970 to 2 per cent in 1994. Romania represented the largest country in volumes in this region, whereas in 1994 just 1.6 billion tonne-kms were transported.

2. PRESENT MARKETS IN WESTERN EUROPE

Geographically speaking, the present markets in western Europe consist of the following:

1.   International axes: the North-South corridor (Netherlands-Belgium-France), the Rhine corridor, the East-West axis (around the Mittelland Canal) and, recently, the Rhine-Main-Danube axis (the South-East corridor);
2.   Domestic transport around the axes mentioned above;
3.   The Finnish market and some smaller, isolated markets.

2.1. North-South corridor

In 1990, the total volume of inland waterway traffic found on the North-South corridor amounted to 133.4 million tonnes. Table 4 presents the Origin/Destination table of inland waterway transport on the North-South corridor for 1990.

Table 4. Inland waterway traffic on the North-South corridor, 1990
(*1 000 tonnes)

	France	Belgium	Netherlands	Total
France	27 194	1 716	1 230	30 140
Belgium	2 463	21 187	12 635	36 286
Netherlands	1 759	31 678	33 546	66 982
Total	31 415	54 581	47 411	133 408

Source: *Analysis of traffic flows within the framework of the Trans-European Inland Waterways Network*, NEA/Planco, 1994.

Around 39 per cent of the total traffic, approximately 52 million tonnes, is international. Most transport is concentrated on the high-capacity links in the Netherlands and Belgium.

About 16 million tonnes is transit traffic, mainly passing through the Netherlands and Belgium.

On the North-South corridor, the largest flows concern building minerals and materials. In addition, solid mineral fuels, fertilisers and oil and oil products make use of inland waterways.

2.2. Rhine corridor

In 1990, about 207 million tonnes of goods were carried on the Rhine corridor. A very high portion of this total volume can be traced back to transport between Germany and the Netherlands and to transport within German territory.

Table 5. **Traffic flows (*1 000 tonnes) on the Rhine corridor (1990)**
Transport mode: Inland water

From/to	Switz.	W. Germ.	Neth.	Belg. & Fr.	Lux.	S-E c.	E-W c.	Total
Switz.	0	171	94	45	0	1	2	313
W. Germ.	2 682	37 260	29 877	12 048	369	2 001	6 420	90 657
Neth.	3 205	68 519	0	4 114	325	1 887	3 339	81 389
Belg. & Fr.	1 577	16 616	3 361	2 371	33	241	1 152	25 351
Lux.	2	565	80	177	0	69	13	906
S-E c.	4	1 080	537	318	0		69	2 008
E-W c.	125	2 942	1 957	1 612	16	179		6 831
Total	7 595	127 153	35 906	20 685	743	4 378	10 995	207 455

Source: Analysis of Traffic Flows Within the Framework of the Trans-European
Inland Waterways Network, NEA/Planco, 1994.

S-E c.   =   South-East corridor
E-W c.   =   East-West corridor.

In 1990, the total transport volume on the Rhine corridor (all modes) was 736 million tonnes. Inland waterway transport and rail transport achieved almost the same modal share (28 per cent each). Therefore, 44 per cent of the total transport volume consisted of road transport.

The bulk of transport of petroleum products, ores, metal waste and fertiliser are carried out by ship. Also a high modal share can be established for the transport of building minerals and materials (43 per cent).

2.3. East-West corridor

In 1990, about 123 million tonnes of goods were carried on the East-West corridor. This total volume can almost exclusively be attributed to transport from and to regions of the Rhine corridor as well as to corridor-internal traffic flows within German regions of the East-West corridor.

One look at inland waterway volumes, broken down to eleven commodity groups in 1990, shows the extraordinary importance of commodity group building minerals and materials, ores and metal waste.

In 1990, the total transport volume on the East-West corridor (all modes) was 505 million tonnes. The modal share of railway transport shows a high rate (36.7 per cent) compared to the share of road transport (39 per cent).

Table 6. **Traffic flows (*1 000 tonnes) on the East-West corridor (1990) Transport mode: Inland water**

From/to	Poland	CSFR	W. Germ.	Rhine c.	South-East c.	Total
Poland	0	0	826	176	0	1 002
Czecho-slovakia	0	0	524	10	22	556
West Germany	25	498	24 838	39 865	1 083	66 309
Rhine corridor	24	23	54 917			54 964
South-East corridor	0	1	269			270
Total	49	522	81 374	40 051	1 105	123 101

Source: Analysis of Traffic Flows Within the Framework of the Trans-European Inland Waterways Network, NEA/Planco, 1994.

2.4. South-East corridor

In 1990, about 11 million tonnes of goods were shipped in the South-East corridor. A high proportion of this can be attributed to transport from and to regions of the Rhine corridor as well as to corridor-internal traffic flows within German regions of the corridor and to traffic flows from Germany to Austria.

Table 7. **Traffic flows (*1 000 tonnes) on the South-East corri[dor]**
Transport mode: Inland water

From/to	Hungary	Romania	Bulgaria	Austria	W. Germ.	Rhine c.	E-W	
Hungary	0	0	0	0	435	0		
Romania	0	0	0	0	133	0	0	155
Bulgaria	0	0	0	0	81	0	0	81
Austria	0	0	0	0	339	0	0	339
W. Germ.	15	56	56	908	2 400	1 939	69	5 443
Rhine c.	0	0	0	0	4 201			4 201
S-E c.	0	0	0	0	178			178
Total	15	56	56	908	7 767	1 939	69	10 810

Source: Analysis of Traffic Flows Within the Framework of the Trans-European
Inland Waterways Network, NEA/Planco, 1994.

The main commodity groups for inland navigation in 1990 are, in order
of importance:

–   metal products (4.2 million tonnes);
–   solid mineral fuels (1.7 million tonnes);
–   petroleum products (1 million tonnes).

In 1990, 163 million tonnes were shipped on the South-East corridor
(all modes). The modal share of road transport is very highly rated compared
to the other corridors, with the exception of the North-South corridor;
it amounts to 65 per cent. For railway transport, a modal share of 29 per cent
can be established.

2.5. Demand analysis

The majority of commodities transported by the inland waterway transport
industry are solid and liquid bulk commodities such as solid mineral fuels,
metal ores, scrap, crude or processed mineral products, building materials,
fertilisers, chemical products (solid and liquid) and oil products.

The transport demand concerning those products is determined by the
structure of the related industry. Therefore, demand predominantly depends on
the economic activities of the related basic industry and their production

.racteristics, for instance, location of the industry, sources of raw material needed, energy consumption, pre-production requirements, work diversification with other national and international industries, kind of output/products. Thus, changes in production procedures will directly affect transportation requirements and therefore determine transport demand.

Of course, this interdependence has to be considered the other way round as well. Locations of various types of industries have been selected according to transport possibilities, e.g. site selection for power plants, steel mills and chemical industries have been influenced by the availability of raw materials such as coal, oil products, iron ores, etc. However, transportation demand is directly influenced by the availability of transport facilities such as pipelines, railways and waterways in the case of bulk goods.

As the bulk of raw materials has to be imported and a considerable share of production is determined for export markets, sea ports create a significant demand as origin or destination of inland waterway transport.

Generally speaking, the development of consumption and production basically determine transportation demand. For aggregated commodity groups, the relevant determinants of demand are listed in Table 8.

A shipper's decision is strongly influenced by the standard of services provided by the available modes of transportation. For the shipper, the attraction of inland waterway transport lies in low freight rates. With respect to bulk goods with relatively low values, this method of transportation should not necessarily be considered as slow.

Although vessels will never be able to equal the speed of railway or pipeline transportation, waterway transportation of these goods does not deserve a reputation of slowness, as long as the pre- and post-shipment stages are taken into consideration. Slowness is not a handicap when one takes into account that inland waterways offer additional low-cost storage capacity. In this context, determinants of demand are, apart from freight costs, safety and regularity of services offered.

Table 8. **General determinants of demand for goods tra**

	Products	Determinants of demand
0	Agricultural products	Production and consumptio agricultural products
1	Food products and fodder	Food production and consu..p....
2	Solid mineral fuels	Mining and quarrying
3	Oil products	Power plants, steel mills, oil industry, energy consumption
4	Metal ores and scrap	Steel mills
5	Metal products	Iron processing industry
6	Crude or processed mineral products, building material	Mining and quarrying, construction industry
7	Fertiliser	Agricultural production
8	Chemical products	Chemical industry
9	Machines, vehicles and manufactured goods	Manufacturing industries

Source: Towards a European Policy for the Inland Waterway Industry, NEA/Planco, 1991.

It must also be recognised that the shipper, as an economic actor, is more or less insensitive to the natural, non-commercial benefits of transportation, such as low macro-economic cost, modest power consumption, beneficial impacts on seaport attractiveness or environmental impacts. He only reacts when production costs are affected by transport costs for supply of raw material or distribution to the market.

Anyway, as far as solid bulky cargoes are concerned, market structures are relatively stable and major changes in demand cannot be expected in the short run, considering the traditional origin and destination relations. Structural changes in the European basis industry, which tends to base production rather on semi-finished products than on raw materials, might affect demand concerning transportation of raw materials such as imported iron ores. Moreover, structural changes in the mining and quarrying industry take place,

189

and possibilities for door-to-door delivery were limited. At present, demand changes slightly, considering transportation time as less relevant than guarantee and reliability of delivery in due time. Waterway transport's chance is to act as part of the transportation chain, compensating higher handling costs with lower transportation costs.

In general, demand can be directed towards waterway transportation by offering adequate transport and handling equipment, efficient organisation of the whole transport chain and by providing suitable information systems. Concerning the hinterland transport of Antwerp and Rotterdam, the waterway transport industry has acted relatively successfully in container transport during the last few years. The implementation of dedicated container terminals along the Rhine has given efficient support to this development.

2.6. The supply side: the enterprise structure

The supply side is dominated by companies comprising 1 or 2 ships, as shown in the following table.

Table 9. **Size of enterprises in inland waterways (1987)**

	Average no. of ships per enterprise	Average tonnage ship	Average tonnage enterprises	% enterprises with 1 or 2 ships	% ships in enterprises with 1 or 2 ships	% tonnage in enterprises with 1 or 2 ships
Belgium	1.24	744	922	97	86	85
Germany	1.66	1 111	1 844	93	60	48
France	1.70	488	829	93	64	54
Netherlands	1.29	911	1 175	96	81	70

Source: Analysis of Traffic Flows within the framework of the Trans-European Inland Waterways Network, NEA/Planco, 1994.

The average number of ships in companies owning at least two ships, is six in Belgium, 6.5 in the Netherlands, nine in France and eleven in Germany. In the larger companies, the average tonnage per ship is higher compared to the smaller companies.

Part of the shipping companies are subsidiaries of organisations in the manufacturing or trading industry, or of larger, usually multimodal, transport conglomerates.

In particular, these companies are connected to the oil, energy, steel and chemical as well as the construction and foodstuffs industries. The characteristic these industries have in common is that they all need or produce huge quantities of relatively low-value goods.

It can be concluded that a fair amount of the shipping companies can be regarded as own-account transporters. Particularly, enterprises with a fleet of more than 20 vessels are linked with industrial organisations. Looking at the situation in Germany, it can be seen that, of this group of enterprises containing less than 1 per cent of the total number of enterprises but operating almost 18 per cent of the vessels and almost 27 per cent of the total tonnage, the vast majority are subsidiaries of industrial organisations. This situation can also be found in the Netherlands, where only 0.2 per cent of the enterprises operate more than 5 per cent of the vessels and almost 11 per cent of the total tonnage.

If one discounts the shipping companies operating as own-account operators, the supply side of the market can be characterised by a very large number of small enterprises (consisting of numerous owner-operators and a few shipping companies) with a small number of vessels and tonnage.

A shipping company which is a subsidiary of an organisation in the industry, is assured of direct access to an important (potential) customer. For the other inland waterway transport organisations, the contacts with the demand side of the market usually follow different, although sometimes similar patterns.

In the IWT sector, there are a number of commercial co-operatives. Here, the situation is referred to in which individual companies jointly approach their clients via one single organisation. In principle, an individual entrepreneur will lose part (or all) of his commercial independence by joining such an organisation on the basis of a medium- or long-term contract. Naturally, he will only be prepared to do so if the co-operation creates an added value to his existence and if he is offered the possibility to participate in the establishment of the common policy.

The spot market plays an important role on the IWT freight market. However, there are parties on the demand side who prefer to come to medium or long-term freight agreements with well-known partners. This usually concerns larger flows on behalf of clients who require an above-average service level, or at least require the certainty that the carrier can take care of an entire transport package. It is obvious that such requirements cannot be fulfilled by an owner-operator on his own. The construction of a commercial co-operation is his only way to obtain direct access to those larger clients and to reduce his dependence on intermediaries.

If well-shaped and managed, the commercial co-operation is able to offer to the demand side the same services as larger shipowning companies, while maintaining ample entrepreneurial freedom for its members. It is a prerequisite, however, that the members truly understand the importance of the service aspect, and manage to make their own (often short-term) interests subordinate to the (long-term) interest of the co-operation.

Although co-operation is not necessarily restricted to that between companies operating the same mode of transport, the remaining part of this section will only discuss co-operation among IWT companies.

The legal form under which the co-operation takes place varies. The most usual forms are limited companies, foundations and co-operative societies. In some of these forms, participation by the members takes place in the joint capital. Another difference in the nature of co-operation is the way in which the members are bound by contract. This concerns matters such as an obligation to accept offered freight under specific circumstances, or a restriction to certain operating areas and/or certain goods, etc.

Differences also exist in the way the commercial co-operative bodies represent the interests of their members. Most of these bodies are involved in marketing and co-ordination of transport tasks and possess the power to enter into agreements. Other activities can be documentation, joint purchasing or even (although seldom) forwarding or transshipment.

The majority of the activities of the commercial co-operative bodies take place on the dry cargo market. Commercial co-operation in the tanker market was recently intensified. Looking at the situation in Germany and the Netherlands, it can be seen that most co-operations involve the transport of cereals and animal fodder, crude and manufactured minerals, solid mineral fuels, iron ore and metal products, fertilizers and general cargo.

The structure of the supply side is one of the causes for the decline in market share of the inland waterway. Functions such as marketing and product development have not been developed in the way they could have been under a different market structure consisting of a larger average firm size.

3. BASIC FORECASTS

Forecasts have been made in the study "Medium/Longterm Forecasts of the Modal Share in Goods Transport Demand". This study was carried out by NEA in 1994 on behalf of DGVII of the European Commission. This study is based on a forecast of the total transport, irrespective of the transport mode used, for the year 2005 with respect to the EU, Austria and Switzerland. Under the scenario used in this study, the overall growth in transport demand in tonnes (all modes) is considered to be 26.7 per cent during the period 1990-2005.

Modal-split functions have been developed for a segmented market using a division between dominant, competitive and restrained markets, based on commodity groups, distance classes and the availibility of infrastructure per mode on specific relations.

For each of these segments, in which a number of origin-destination relations are grouped, a modal-share function is estimated, in which the share of inland waterways is explained by the ratio of transport tariffs and times relative to other modes, and to the total transport.

For the share of each transport mode, a modal-share function is estimated, resulting in a share function for each segment and each mode. A change in relative tariffs and times does not have an effect on one mode only, but it also results in changes in the share of the other competitive inland modes, depending on the parameters found in that specific segment. The effects of the changes in the modal share should balance.

It should be realised that this segmented representation of the transport market does not equate with a series of uniform transport mode situations, as there is still a wide variety of modal shares, even within each market segment.

Nevertheless, it is considered that there is more homogeneity between the relations falling within a market segment than within the total transport market for that commodity, as shown by the reduction in the variance of the modal share. The specific values of the transport-service variables used in the modal-choice functions for each market segment are assumed to provide a reasonable, although not exhaustive, representation of the performance of the transport modes. The hypothesis is that this measurement of the quality of the transport service for each mode within each market segment will enable the determinants of modal choice to be isolated and expressed in terms of a modal-share function. The significance of each transport-service variable within this function will provide insights into the relative influence of each variable in the modal-choice process.

For the future competitive position between the modes, the following assumptions have been made.

3.1. Rail transport

The continuation of the development of railway tariffs could be quantified due to the Transport Markets Observation documents published by the European Commission.

During the period 1981-88, in six Member States of the Community (Benelux, Germany, France, Italy) a yearly average rise of railway tariffs of 4.06 per cent was recorded, with a considerable decrease at the end of this period. The percentage recorded in the period 1988-89, 2.46 per cent, has been taken for the period 1990-2005, which amounts to a factor of 1.44 for the whole period.

3.2. Inland waterway transport

In the period 1982-90, the tariffs valid in inland waterway transport markets have seen a stable development with a very small rise over the entire period. The increase in tariffs was estimated by the Commission at 1.1 per cent a year, for both Rhine transport (dry cargo) and North-South transport (Netherlands-Belgium-northern France). From the excess capacity in the market, it appears that the tariffs do not cover the costs.

It was assumed that this situation could not last in the long term: the EU policy of barge scrapping was designed to reduce the excess capacity so that the outcome is an increase in tariffs and the equilibrium is restored.

However, this policy did not have the intended effect. The thought is justified that, in the long term, the tariffs should rise faster than was the case in the past. This overtaking manoeuvre is intended to reduce, between 1990 and 2010, the observed difference in 1989 of 36 per cent between costs and tariffs. The tariffs will rise in the period 1990-2005 with a factor of 1.49.

3.3. Road transport

As far as road transport services are concerned, the Commission registered a yearly average rise of tariffs of 2.11 per cent during the period 1982-90. In the period 1986-90, this figure decreased to 1.3 per cent. It is very likely that in a liberalised market the tariffs of road transport will slightly rise, which did happen in the recent past: the gain in productivity can compensate for the increase in wages. Therefore, the rise in tariffs has been estimated to be 1.3 per cent a year between 1990 and 2005, which is lower than the average rise in the general price level during this period. This results in a factor of 1.21 for this period.

In the establishment of the expected changes in tariffs of multimodal transport, of which rail and inland waterway are the main conveyors, the change in the cost of handling and transshipment to/from the road should be accounted for. Also the cost of front and end haulage should be included. It is assumed that the transshipment cost follows the increase in the general consumption price index.

In line with the economic development in Europe, economic growth goes hand in hand with an increase in the consumption price index of 3.94 per cent a year in the EU. For the period 1990-2005, this means a factor of 1.79.

Moreover, the following list of actual policy measures has been included in the analysis, which is mainly focused on road transport:

- Free access to domestic transport markets;
- Abolition of customs formalities;
- Harmonization of road taxes;
- Harmonization of fuel taxes;
- Introduction of environmental taxes;
- Road-use taxation schemes;
- Speed limitation;
- Harmonization of weights and measures;
- Harmonization of VAT.

In Table 10, the main results are given for the year 2005; in Table 11, they are given as an index based on the year 1990.

196

It can be observed in Table 10 that in 2005 about 53 per cent of total transport (6.4 billion tonnes) is intra-regional within the EU, the modal split of which is more or less invariant to exogenous cost changes and policy measures. Nearly all intra-regional transport is moved by road. Though the share of intra-regional transport is large, it must be stated that the transport distances in this case are shorter, so that measured in performance (tonne-kms) its share becomes much smaller.

Table 10. **Transport by mode in 2005 in 1 000 tonnes for inter- and intraregional domestic transport and international transport in relation with the EU and transport in other regions**

	Other modes	Road	Rail	IWT	Sea	Total	%
EU domestic/ intra	0	6 210 792	149 016	73 235	0	6 433 044	52.72
EU domestic/ inter	0	1 915 975	343 804	93 895	232 169	2 585 842	21.19
International trade within the EU	97 562	411 097	64 538	126 938	242 724	942 859	7.73
EU trade with non-Community countries	328 400	350 319	179 318	197 759	870 769	1 926 564	15.79
EU total	425 961	8 888 182	736 677	491 827	1 345 662	11 888 309	97.43
Austria & Switz.	5 466	226 831	58 369	4 448	18 872	313 986	2.57
Total	431 427	9 115 013	795 046	496 275	1 364 534	12 202 295	100.0
%	3.54	74.70	6.52	4.07	11.18	100.0	

Source: Medium/Longterm Forecasts of the Modal Share in Goods Transport Demand, NEA, 1994.

Table 11 shows the forces underlying the modal-split development. Inland waterways have to bear a significant loss in the domestic transport between regions. Some of the loss, on the other hand, is regained in trade of non-Community countries, where in most transit-transport cases one side of the transport chain in Europe consists of inland waterway transport (for goods such as animal feed, ores, fertilizers, chemicals, etc.).

Table 11. **Index of transport by mode in 2005 (1990=100) for inter- and intra-regional domestic transport and international transport in relation with the EU and transport in other regions**

	Other modes	Road	Rail	IWT	Sea	Total
EU domestic/intra	-	125.4	106.0	124.3	-	124.9
EU domestic/inter	-	125.4	123.1	88.3	117.4	122.5
International trade With EU	139.0	149.2	127.1	105.2	137.4	135.9
EU trade with non-Community countries	126.6	149.1	181.4	136.3	127.2	135.4
Austria & Switzerland	118.0	120.8	133.0	222.8	168.8	125.9
Total	129.1	127.0	129.6	114.6	127.5	126.7

Source: Medium/Longterm Forecasts of the Modal Share in Goods Transport Demand, NEA, 1994.

In Tables 12 and 13, the modal share per commodity group in 1990 and 2005 is given. A comparison between Tables 12 and 13 shows that inland waterway transport is confronted with a generally small decrease in share in the modal split for all commodity groups. Inland waterway transport, such as rail transport, is faced with tariff-determining factors which are not limited to the inland waterway transport market but which influence the total tariff from origin to destination, i.e. transshipment costs and costs of front and end haulage. However, in the case of inland waterways, the basic tariffs are assumed to grow more than for road and rail. This is the effect of policy assumptions which suppose that, in the long term, tariffs should be in harmony with costs, which means an additional increase in tariffs. This context proves the importance of choice of policy measures.

One exception is the increase in the share of metal products. The explanation for this fact is that inland waterways benefit from the increase of the total demand of metal products. This phenomenon, the so-called volume effect, compensates the negative effect of higher growth of inland-waterway tariffs.

It is clear that under assumptions where the inland waterway tariffs will rise less compared to railways, the growth of inland waterway transport will exceed the 15 per cent in 15 years calculated in this study. However, such effects will be limited, since price competition exists only in a limited number of market segments.

A study carried out by NEA and Planco in 1994 on four corridors showed higher increases for IWT for the year 2010: compared to 1990, 28 per cent on the North-South axis, 29 per cent on the Rhine axis, 66 per cent on the East-West axis and 64 per cent on the South-East axis. This is mainly the result from an optimistic economic scenario; in this forecast, the modal share of IWT on all four axes is also slightly decreasing.

Table 12. **Modal share per commodity group in 1990 in percentages, Interregional transport**

	Other modes	Road	Rail	IWT	Sea	Total
Agricultural products	1.9	69.5	9.0	5.2	14.3	100.0
Foodstuffs	3.9	75.5	4.2	5.3	11.2	100.0
Solid mineral fuels	4.3	12.7	28.8	15.7	38.6	100.0
Crude oil	25.9	1.8	0.5	1.3	70.5	100.0
Ores and minerals	6.1	13.3	20.0	22.5	38.0	100.0
Metal products	0.6	52.3	25.8	6.8	14.4	100.0
Building materials	0.7	62.4	8.7	18.1	10.1	100.0
Fertilizer	2.5	44.4	14.9	13.9	24.5	100.0
Chemical products	2.6	62.3	10.8	8.0	16.1	100.0
Machines, vehicles and Manufactured goods	1.1	79.2	8.5	0.6	10.7	100.0
Petroleum products	26.3	17.3	7.9	12.8	35.7	100.0
Total	7.9	48.1	10.1	8.8	25.1	100.0

Source: Medium/Longterm Forecasts of the Modal Share in Goods Transport Demand, NEA, 1994.

Table 13. **Modal share per commodity group in 2005 in percentages, Interregional transport**

	Other modes	Road	Rail	IWT	Sea	Total
Agricultural products	2.3	66.2	11.8	4.6	15.1	100.0
Foodstuffs	3.9	71.8	6.4	5.1	12.8	100.0
Solid mineral fuels	4.2	13.4	29.0	14.1	39.2	100.0
Crude oil	25.9	1.8	0.5	1.3	70.5	100.0
Ores and minerals	6.0	14.1	20.7	21.3	37.9	100.0
Metal products	0.7	48.9	27.1	8.4	15.0	100.0
Building materials	0.7	65.5	9.0	14.0	10.7	100.0
Fertilizer	2.7	44.7	15.8	11.4	25.4	100.0
Chemical products	2.9	59.6	12.5	7.7	17.2	100.0
Machines, vehicles and Manufactured goods	1.2	77.7	9.2	0.6	11.4	100.0
Petroleum products	26.6	15.2	6.8	11.6	39.8	100.0
Total	7.9	49.0	10.7	7.7	24.7	100.0

Source: Medium/Longterm Forecasts of the Modal Share in Goods Transport Demand, NEA, 1994.

4. POLICY TOWARDS INLAND WATERWAY TRANSPORT

Recently, it became obvious that if policies towards the transport markets are continued as in the past, the growth of road freight transport will be higher than desired, seen from an environmental point of view, causing high energy consumption and pollution. Moreover, such growth causes undesired developments in land use. In both national and European green and white papers, a new approach has been proposed and in some cases adopted, leading to a more sustainable development. In these papers, the promotion of environment-friendly modes is always an important item. Besides the promotion of railways and inland waterways, there is also short sea transport; the promotion of combined transport is seen as an attractive solution.

Although this change in approach has been announced for over ten years, up to now the effect on the modal split has been limited. The liberation in the road transport sector has improved its competitive position. Moreover, the instruments to influence modal split have not produced the required effect.

The main causes are as follows:

– The market is strongly segmented and road transport has a dominant position in many segments; moreover, markets in which road transport is dominant are generally growing faster than bulk markets;
– The railways are in a position of transition towards commercially operating companies, but do meet several problems to reach this stage. One of these problems is the lack of technical integration in international operations;
– The structure of supply of the intermodal market was insufficient to allow a major shift towards combined transport;
– There is a lack of innovative and marketing forces in large parts of the inland waterway sector.

Nevertheless, it is still a main objective of transport policy to influence the modal split; new and more refined instruments to achieve this are being studied and are partly being prepared. In the paper "Towards a fair and efficient pricing", the theory on marginal pricing including external effects has been introduced and many countries are prepared to introduce road pricing as an instrument for implementation. In combined transport, stronger attempts will be made to reduce the costs of terminal handling and to improve the quality. Infrastructure bottlenecks in railways, inland waterway and terminal access and capacity have priority.

On the other hand, measures to improve traffic management in road transport are taken, often giving priority to economically important (freight) transport in relation to economically less important traffic. In addition, the completion of a European system of autoroutes makes road transport more attractive.

As a result, measures to improve the supply side of IWT are very important. Only a combination of instruments on pricing with improvements on the supply side can lead to the realisation of a shift towards IWT.

5. POTENTIALS

In 1994, NEA and Planco carried out a study for the European Commission, DGVII, called "Analysis of Traffic Flows within the Framework of the Trans-European Inland Waterways Network". In this study, the potential for IWT maintained a broad approach using the principle of transport chains. A transport chain is defined as a chain of successive transport modes to carry a certain good from its first origin to its final destination. Along the chain, a number of transshipments may take place at certain points.

The potential on a corridor is achieved by combining three approaches:

–   The first approach is merely through the effect of a change in tariffs on the modal shares. This approach starts from the actual modal split in a given year and uses price cross-elasticities between the modes to calculate the impact of small tariff changes on the modal split. Accordingly, this approach is called the "elasticity potential".

–   The second approach works from an average modal split for origin and destination flows that are being served by inland waterway transport. The assumption is that the potential is determined not so much by prices as by the organisation of the transportation market, so that comparable modal splits can be found in markets with comparable characteristics. For this purpose, the market is segmented according to distance class and commodity group.

One of the main reasons for using the second approach is that the proposed change in tariffs is not the only force determining the potential. Imponderable factors such as organisation of the market and even the image of the modes, have an impact on the modal split. This second approach will be referred to as the "target potential".

–   The first two approaches described above concentrate on the transport flows found on the corridor. The third approach has a broader scope and concentrates on those transport flows partly or fully outside the corridor and the inland waterway network. Where the first two approaches rely on tariff changes and/or the organisation of the transport market, the third approach concentrates entirely on the organisation of the transport markets. The third approach is the "shifting potential".

Within the chain concept, the strength of terminals is important. The strengths or weaknesses of an inland waterway terminal largely depend on the extent to which the terminal is able to meet the demands of the combined transport company/inland waterway shipping company, which in their turn should also meet the demands of the transport company (logistical service provider). The latter offers a range of transport services which fit in with the logistical chain of the shipper with regard to his customers. The better a terminal provides a suitable range of services to the combined transport company/shipping company/road transport company, the stronger its position will be in the combined transport chain, especially when taking into account that, compared with road and rail, over longer distances, inland waterway transport is very competitive from an economic point of view.

In the near future, this competitive position of inland waterway transport could improve for the following reasons.

In January 1992, the Montbazon Agreement was abolished. This means that the division between continental and maritime combined transport has ceased to exist. The consequence of this is already becoming clear. Increased competition between the various parties on the market is becoming apparent, especially between the multimodal transport companies and railway companies, but also between the multimodal transport companies and maritime shipping companies. Furthermore, due to the disappearance of the market segmentation, terminals can also play a role in both former market segments: in continental as well as in maritime combined transport.

A long-term improvement in combined transport is expected as a result of the modification of Directive 75/130/EEC by Directive 91/224/EEC of 27 March 1991, which came into force on 1 January 1992.

These modifications concern the following three elements:

–   Road transport: the initial or final road transport leg of an international combined transport service shall be accessible to any carrier from any EC Member State who complies with the demands for entering the market between the States. The Directive also applies even where the link does not include a border;

–   Inland waterway transport: the maximum distance to or from the port of loading or unloading has been increased from 50 to 150 kilometres;

–   Own-account transport link: a consignee will be able to use the trailer or semi-trailer of an own-account operator for the terminal-road transport link of a combined transport consignment. The opposite also applies.

Using this approach, forecasts have been made for the year 2010, using PROGNOS economic forecasts as a basis, with an estimated growth of GDP in the EU of 2.8 per cent a year between 1990 and 2010.

5.1. North-South axis

On the North-South axis, the total volume carried by inland waterways, as a basic forecast, will have risen by 28 per cent to 170 million tonnes. French domestic traffic by IWT will drop by 12 per cent, and French exports will also show a considerable decline. French imports from the Netherlands will increase by 28 per cent, rising to almost 2.3 million tonnes.

A large increase of 72 per cent is found in the exports from the Netherlands to Belgium, growing to a total flow of 55.2 million tonnes in 2010.

The differences in growth figures on the various relations by inland waterways are largely explained by the changes in commodity groups carried. For example, domestic inland waterways in France carry a high volume of crude minerals and building materials. The expected cost increases in inland waterways as well as the free capacity on rail make rail into a competitive alternative.

A comparison with other modes of transport gives an indication of the competitiveness of inland waterways. The total transport volume on the corridor is 1.4 billion tonnes. In 1990, inland waterways had a modal share of 10 per cent. With a modal share of 84 per cent, road transport was by far the most important means of transport, whereas only 5.3 per cent was carried by rail.

In 2010, the total volume carried will have risen to 2 billion tonnes. Even though the volume of inland waterways grows from 133 to 170 million tonnes, the modal share of inland waterways is declining to 8.5 per cent. In 2010, road and rail will have modal shares of 84 per cent and 7.5 per cent respectively.

Compared to other modes, inland waterways carry mainly solid mineral fuels as well as oil and oil products. Here, inland waterways had a modal share of from 29 to 35 per cent in 1990, increasing to 44 per cent in 2010 in the case of solid mineral fuels.

The lowest share of the market held by inland waterways is found for machinery and manufactured products. Even though the transport of manufactured products will be more than doubled, with 300 million tonnes in 2010, the absolute volume carried by inland waterways will drop from 1.9 to 1.6 million tonnes, leaving a modal share of only 0.6 per cent.

In the sector of building minerals and materials, the absolute volume carried by inland waterways also shows a decline, resulting in a decrease in modal share from 10 per cent to only 6.7 per cent. In contrast to this can be seen the development of road transport, increasing its modal share from 56 per cent to 90 per cent in 2010.

The "target potential" of the North-South corridor has been established by assuming that most favourable market conditions on each corridor would lead to average modal shares of inland waterways for each link. This is done by classifying each relationship according to a market segmentation depending on distance class and commodity group. The average modal shares by segment are those observed in 1990 and estimated for 2010 for interregional transport in Europe. They constitute a target as long as they have not been measured on the origin x destination relation considered.

The effect of price changes in inland waterways transport on the North-South corridor is relatively moderate. The volume of transport captured from other modes as a result of price reductions of 10 per cent to 30 per cent is given in Table 14 below.

The total volume of 170 million tonnes of inland waterways in the reference scenario can be expanded by some 0.15 million tonnes by cutting prices by 30 per cent.

The target potential is estimated at an additional 88 million tonnes in 2010, showing that, in a situation in which the organisation of the inland waterways is optimised, a total volume of 258 million tonnes is attainable. The shifting potential is even much higher.

Table 14. Elasticity potential (*1 000 tonnes)

	Price change IWT		
	10%	20%	30%
1990 *captured from:*			
• Rail	3 589	5 809	7 783
• Road	1 506	2 879	4 097
Total	5 095	8 688	11 880
2010 *captured from:*			
• Rail	4 037	6 673	8 385
• Road	2 131	4 074	6 101
Total	6 168	10 747	14 486

Source: Analysis of traffic flows within the framework of the Trans-European Inland Waterways Network, NEA/Planco, 1994.

5.2. The Rhine axis

On the Rhine axis, the basic forecasting data of 2010 show that the total transport volume by IWT will increase by 29 per cent to 267 million tonnes. This growth will be mainly attributed to a large increase in inland waterways freight shipped between the East-West corridor and German regions belonging to the Rhine corridor. Furthermore, exports from Belgium and France to German regions of the Rhine corridor will be chiefly responsible for the increasing transport volume on this corridor.

Only rail will be able to increase its modal share in 2010. According to the forecast, nearly one-third of all transport on this corridor will be carried out by train. The modal share of inland waterway transport will decrease to 26 per cent. The modal share of road transport will also decline slightly, to 42 per cent.

The bulk of transport of petroleum products, ores, metal waste and fertilizer are carried out by ship. Also, inland waterways take a high modal share in the transport of building minerals and materials (43 per cent). Although they will slightly decline in importance, in 2010, the inland waterway

206

will still be the most important transport mode for these commodity groups. Moreover, the corresponding transport volumes will increase between 1990 and 2010.

For the Rhine corridor, the potential generally available for transshipment to inland waterway transport has been identified by isolating railway and road transport between sub-regions with direct access to the inland waterway network. This potential is supposed to present the volumes that can be tackled by organisational, regulative and price-political activities of the inland waterway transport industry.

In this case, the shifting potential in 2010 represents an additional 443 million tonnes for the northern part of the corridor and 267 million tonnes for the southern part. The target potential can be stated as 30 per cent of the shifting potential.

5.3. Other axes

On the East-West axis and the South-East corridor, the approaches have been similar to those on the Rhine corridor, as is shown by the results:

Table 15. **Basic forecasts 2010 and shifting potential of IWT (million tonnes)**

	1990	**2010 basic forecasts**	**2010 shifting potential**
East-West corridor	123	204	510
South-East corridor	11	18	98

Source: Analysis of traffic flows within the framework of the Trans-European Inland Waterways Network, NEA/Planco, 1994.

Compared to the reference situation, a shift potential has been derived, consisting of all road and rail transport that has access to the inland waterway network. In the reference situation, IWT on the Rhine corridor captures about 30 per cent of the total shift potential. On the North-South corridor and the

South-East corridor, these percentages are 19 per cent and 15 per cent respectively. This indicates that on the North-South corridor and the South-East corridor IWT is relatively underdeveloped. It appears that the high-capacity links in the northern parts of each corridor have realised the highest actual transport volumes and the lowest additional shift potential. The largest relative growth can be expected on the southern, least developed parts of the network, even though substantial upgrading of the networks might be necessary.

It is obvious that, in case the target potential is defined as 30 per cent of the shifting potential, the increase will be very substantial. On the other hand, the conditions for achieving this potential are not easy to realise. The primary condition is an IWT and a combined IWT/road transport industry operating on a fully commercial and innovative basis. However, although the target of 30 per cent of the shift potential is perhaps overambitious, the outcomes of the study are challenging.

6. AN EXAMPLE: CONTAINERS ON THE RHINE

The introduction, in the mid-sixties, of the maritime container in the intercontinental transport of general cargo caused inland waterway transport to lose a significant market share in the inland transport of this goods flow. In the second half of the seventies, a number of enterprises succeeded in professionalising and developing container transport on the Rhine. By now, figures have proved that inland navigation is making a serious comeback: its share in the container flow between the Europoort area and Germany has grown from 5 per cent in 1978 to nearly 35 per cent in 1993. During that same period, the share of rail transport decreased from 20 per cent to 3 per cent. The remaining part was taken up by road transport. The total container flow to the German hinterland doubled in that period to approximately 800 000 containers.

On the Rhine, some dozen barge operators are active. If so required, they take full responsibility for inland transport, in a seaport-to-door package of services, including transshipment on the inland terminal and the connecting road transport in pre- and end haulage. To an increasing extent, additional logistic services are also on offer. The barge operators work partly in association in order to increase operational efficiency and fill in possible gaps in their individual areas of operation.

At the moment, the operators bring some sixty, mostly chartered, ships into service on the Rhine. This young fleet is extended at high speed with even larger units that are even better attuned to container navigation. Whereas in 1980 mostly 90-TEU (TEU = Twenty-foot Equivalent Unit) ships sailed, now increasingly more 200-TEU ships and motor vessel/pushbarge combinations with a capacity of 350 TEU (200 for the pushing vessel and 150 for the pushbarge) are put into action. The average is now at about 160 TEU. This is an indication of the room for the economies of scale that can still be realised. The sixty ships represent a mere one per cent of the whole of the Rhine fleet. Expansion of capacity is therefore not at all a problem for container barge operations.

The chartered ships are usually the property of independent entrepreneurs who own one or two ships. They are the ones that show the courage to invest in the necessary specialised fleet units. Through them, the sector combines the economic advantages of a small enterprise in the area of execution with the power of the operators' logistic, commercial and management capacities on shore.

In the Rhine basin between Rotterdam and Basel, 32 full container terminals are available. Most of these have rail connections at their disposal, even though their use is insubstantial. Frequently carried out regular services, with fixed departure schedules, connect the terminals in the hinterland with the seaport terminals in Rotterdam, Antwerp and Amsterdam. Several times a day, the main terminals are called at. On average, the joint operators offer a departure from Rotterdam every 2.5 hours.

The inland container ships are suitable for all occurring containers, including deviant sizes, reefer containers, as well as containers with dangerous substances.

6.1. The market

Both shippers and sea shipping companies can act as clients for the hinterland transport of maritime containers. They form two separate market segments, respectively called Merchant Haulage and Carrier Haulage. Large shippers tend more and more to take the control for hinterland transport upon themselves, or to have this transport directed by their forwarding agent. Inland navigation is prominent in both markets. This makes it necessary for container barge operations to operate very cautiously and to maintain strict neutrality with regard to both clients who sometimes compete with each other.

To an increasing extent, container barge operations transport high-quality products such as electronics, machine parts, foodstuffs and chemical products. It may count on large and renowned enterprises for its clients.

Container barge operations, by their very nature, offer intermodal transport: additional transport by road or rail is virtually always necessary to reach a final destination. Accordingly, in Rhine container navigation there is good co-operation between the barge operators and local road transport companies, who complete the transport chain to some 100 to 150 km from the Rhine terminals.

In 1993, over 800 000 containers, empty and loaded, were transported between Rotterdam and Germany. Of this amount, inland navigation transported over 250 000, which is a share of almost 35 per cent. Of the total amount, 80 per cent concerns the Rhine regions. In these regions, inland navigation transported over 40 per cent of the tonnes carried in containers, and the railways 2 per cent; the remaining nearly 60 per cent were transported by road.

This still young branch of industry is working on a strengthening of its structure. It is expected that the operators will come to a more intensive operational collaboration, while retaining their commercial identity and independence. Ever more means of production are combined, as is done in sea transport, which can lead to, among other things, an optimum attunement of sailing schedules.

In addition to a continuing ship innovation, the branch also works on technology improvements in the field of container transshipment and telematics. Particularly the latter is considered to be essential for a better harmonization of demand and supply, in order to be able to further optimise the handling of container transport by inland navigation.

Apart from these internal actions, there are also external developments which offer opportunities for optimisation. Both in Rotterdam and in the hinterland, a concentration of terminals can be expected. In Rotterdam, a further concentration of transshipment on the *Maasvlakte* is taking place. Expectations are that in the hinterland the accent will be on a smaller number than the current 32 terminals, of a higher-quality nature and at an optimum distance from one another.

7. CONCLUSION

Although declining in relative share, the traditional markets of IWT are still growing in absolute figures. The underlying process here is a general tendency towards higher-value goods and a relatively slow development of economic sectors with a high share of IWT.

The developments foreseen in road transport will inevitably lead to a policy which supports the more environment-friendly modes. Especially in intermodal transport, there is a huge potential for IWT.

In order to realise a strong position on these new markets a series of conditions have to be fullfilled:

- The supply structure has to be adapted and become more innovative and market-oriented;
- The techniques and organisation in terminal handling in intermodal transport have to be improved;
- The internalising of external costs in road transport has to be realised.

The main gain of market share is to be achieved in competition with road transport, and marketing and organisation in IWT is to be competitive with this sector. In relation to rail transport, there is less to gain, seeing that:

- the market share of IWT in markets having rail as their main competitor is already high;
- the competitive position of rail transport is expected to improve by introducing competition in the rail sector and by large investments in this sector.

As a result, *intermodal* will be the keyword for future developments in inland waterways. In intermodal transport, the other modes are both partners as well as competitors. Just how far things will develop depends on the organisational potential in the IWT sector.

SUMMARY OF DISCUSSIONS

SUMMARY

The history of inland waterway transport dates back several centuries. The railways were the first mode of transport to provide competition for the inland waterways. Although faster than the latter, they were also more expensive. Road transport subsequently became the dominant mode of transport, easily outstripping its two rivals. Road transport now accounts for the bulk of short-distance traffic and for a substantial share of interregional or international traffic.

The statistics for average growth in freight transport in tonne-kilometres over the period 1970-95 show that road transport has grown by an average 4 per cent a year, whereas growth in the inland waterways sector has remained stagnant and rail transport has declined at a rate of over 1 per cent a year. In terms of the modal split for the three major "inland" modes, all markets combined, the inland waterways are ranked third in Europe after the railways, with the road sector in first place.

At present, the most notable aspect of the inland waterway sector is the large number of small operators, despite the fact that part of the market (transport services on the Rhine) has been liberalised for many years. However, by the year 2000, the entire inland waterway market in the European Union will be liberalised with the abolition of the chartering by rotation system, originally introduced to ensure that goods were carried at a fixed tariff. From the year 2000 onwards, transport prices and conditions will be determined by the forces of supply and demand. Will the inland waterways be able to attract new customers and thus put an end to the now firmly entrenched trend decline in this mode of transport?

The Round Table set out to answer this question by approaching the issue in three stages:

-- Analysis of past trends;
-- Examination of potential markets;
-- Determination of possible policy measures.

1. PAST TRENDS

In European countries other than the former planned economies, the volume of transport services supplied by the inland waterway sector remained virtually unchanged, with waterway activity up from base 100 in 1970 to 110 in 1995. During this period, however, the transport market as a whole experienced very strong growth, practically doubling in size, mainly to the advantage of road haulage. Nonetheless, it is worth noting that, everywhere other than in France, growth in waterway transport outstripped that in rail transport. In France, the breakdown of traffic by type of good has shifted significantly and, in particular, the market for the transport of construction materials has completely collapsed.

Again in relation to the waterways, it should be noted that the situation in many countries was more satisfactory with regard to international transport than to domestic transport. The average distance over which goods were carried has increased, thereby proving that the internationalisation of transport services has also affected the inland waterway sector.

Waterway transport in the CEECs went into sharp decline in 1989 as a result not only of the slump in industrial production and trade but also the halting of river-borne traffic on the Danube due to the crisis in the former Yugoslavia and the resultant embargo on trade. The waterways were also affected by structural changes in the economy, which reduced flows of raw materials and bulk products. In addition, the vessel fleet was disrupted by shortages of spare parts, with the result that vessels were often forced to remain idle.

What is the reason for the relatively poor performance of the waterways in western Europe?

The waterways are eminently suited to the transport of goods whose production has fallen sharply as a result of the industrial restructuring which has taken place in all developed countries. The transport of raw materials, construction materials and products of first-stage processing has been affected by the restructuring of heavy industry and the crisis in the construction sector. This structural effect accounts for about 60 per cent of waterway traffic losses in Germany. The remaining 40 per cent is due to the waterways' lack of competitiveness in traditional markets. The waterways have also had to contend with increased competition from pipelines (particularly after the NATO pipelines, originally built for purely military purposes, entered the market),

218

which explains the sharp fall in the transport of petroleum products. Furthermore, development of the sector is constrained by the low density of the inland waterway network and the slowness of deliveries remains a problem.

Transport market analyses show that, in the past, transport users opted for logistical systems which could guarantee the speed, reliability, availability and flexibility of transport. As a result, the waterways were penalised because they were slow and because the chartering by rotation system failed to meet all the requirements for flexibility imposed by freight charterers. In fact, demand remains high for the transport of high-quality goods and even for bulk products.

Operators could argue that the waterways were the least expensive mode of transport once goods had been loaded onto vessels. But this was not necessarily the main criterion for charterers. Of course, speed and just-in-time requirements vary according to type of good and there is perhaps a tendency to exaggerate the importance of speed in modal choice. Slowness is not necessarily a handicap if account is taken of the fact that the waterways can provide cheap storage capacity. The markets are broken up, however, according to different logistical requirements as well as by geographical area. Until now, therefore, it has been difficult to integrate the waterways into the most advanced forms of logistical organisation, which still remain the preserve of the road sector. However, with the economic crisis, charterers are becoming increasingly sensitive to transport costs and in many cases low unit-value goods such as certain types of agricultural produce, or even heavy bulk materials such as sand or gravel, are uneconomical to ship by road.

Furthermore, it is a fact that, as economic agents, charterers are not fully aware of the natural advantages and thus the non-commercial benefits of transport by inland waterway: low energy consumption, higher safety levels, low macroeconomic costs, an environmentally friendly mode of transport, services that can enhance the attractiveness of maritime ports.

2. POTENTIAL MARKETS

On the whole, the future of the waterways lies more in new markets than in the spin-offs from possible changes in the current modal split. A more aggressive marketing policy would open up larger numbers of outlets for inland waterway transport services, both in new markets and in traditional markets such as bulk solids or liquids, solid mineral fuels, metal ores, scrap metal, refined or unrefined ores, building materials, fertilisers or chemicals and petroleum products.

Many countries have experienced significant growth in the transport by inland waterway of products not normally carried by that mode. These are goods of relatively high value (agricultural produce or foodstuffs, chemicals, machinery, vehicles and manufactured goods). The use of containers should make it possible for the waterways to meet these new types of demand more effectively as well as offering waterways the possibility of playing a role in markets for which they would ostensibly appear to be unsuited.

There can be no denying the fact that continual industrial restructuring and fierce competition in markets for manufactured goods, as a result of globalisation, will lead to the constant reorganisation of logistical chains, thus offering opportunities for the waterways in the future.

Waterway transport can be integrated into logistical chains in which regular flows of supplies and low costs are more important than speed. The nature of demand has changed and it would be fair to say that transport times are now less important than the guarantee of regular and reliable services. When a container ship from the Far East has spent more than twenty days at sea, an additional transport leg of one or two days makes little difference. The salvation of the waterways lies in their integration into transport systems in which increased handling costs can be offset by lower transport costs. The use of waterways to link maritime shipping to final delivery would seem to be perfectly obvious. This sea/waterway interface is already important in ports such as Antwerp and Rotterdam, given that most raw materials have to be imported and that a substantial share of domestic production is destined for export. While the market associated with maritime transport is very buoyant, it would seem that in practical terms it is sometimes difficult to establish a sea/waterway transport interface due to the fragmented nature of supply in the waterway sector. Maritime operators do not always instinctively think of the waterways and inland navigation is often penalised by port practices.

Apart from the waterways in the Russian Federation, Belarus and the Ukraine, there are two major river corridors in Europe: the Rhine and the Danube. The Rhine will continue to be a major corridor in the future, due to qualitative progress in the handling of traffic flows. The share of manufactured goods in these flows is gradually rising and, in addition to this growth, coal transport services have generally started to recover.

Living standards in eastern European countries will rise and the integration of these countries into the world economy should accelerate, thus stimulating growth in traffic flows. There would therefore appear to be very strong potential for growth in traffic in the areas neighbouring on the Black Sea and the Baltic. The outlook for transport in the Russian Federation network also seems promising. However, flows in the Russian Federation, Belarus and Ukraine are unbalanced: exports are mainly composed of agricultural produce and raw materials, while imports primarily consist of industrial goods. Growth in waterway/maritime transport and feeder traffic on the import side should equally be taken into account, while raw material and agricultural exports can also be carried by waterway. It should be noted that river and sea shipping, on the other hand, offers major scope for development, notably in the Baltic and along the Danube.

Traffic on the Danube should grow substantially, given that the Danube can serve as an intermediate link for trade between Europe and central Asia in emerging markets. The Danube also offers a good compromise between transport costs and delivery times on a large number of links. While, admittedly, transport times are slower than by rail, transport costs are much lower. However, scheduled services need to be put in place on the lower reaches of the river to ensure that the services offered are attractive; indeed, such services are a prerequisite in the case of container transport.

Growth in traffic on the Rhine may be fuelled by a marked increase in waterway traffic between the East-West corridor and the German regions on the Rhine corridor. Exports from Belgium and France to the German regions on the Rhine corridor will also contribute to growth.

The future for waterway transport is all the more secure in that it will be difficult for road transport to absorb the very strong growth forecast in goods traffic; the road transport market, however, is relatively distinct from the waterway market. It is also a fact that congestion in the road network, which is particularly severe in the vicinity of ports, will act as a brake on growth in road traffic. Nonetheless, success in the waterway sector is contingent on the ability of operators to both attract and retain customers, and the latter cannot afford to take anything for granted even in the case of apparently captive markets. Bulk freight and raw materials carried by tanker vessels are a traditional market for the inland waterways. New market shares can still be won, provided that operators can offer appropriate equipment and services. It would certainly be to the operators' advantage to create regular multi-customer services for bulk transport by setting up regional port facilities specialised in this type of activity. There is also potential for growth in the transport of dangerous goods.

In general, the waterways can attract custom provided that they can offer appropriate transport and handling equipment, a thoroughly efficient logistical transport chain and efficient information systems. There has been substantial growth in waterway transport in the Antwerp and Rotterdam hinterland, partly as a result of the construction of container terminals along the Rhine. Container transport is also a promising market. However, with regard to the latter, the waterways are primarily used for the repositioning of empty containers, since the transport times for empty containers are less penalising than those for containers loaded with high unit-value goods.

Potential markets with particularly good prospects for waterways also include the transport of refuse, recycling material and imported coal.

Another market which may assume greater importance is the traffic to and from built-up areas and major construction sites, which could attract interest in the light of the Berlin example quoted at the Round Table. As shown by that example, it is possible to use the waterways to bring in large volumes of construction materials and remove rubble which would otherwise be carried by road and therefore cause considerable environmental disturbance. However, steps must be taken to ensure that quayside service areas are not eroded through real estate speculation or attempts to achieve short-term savings which might ultimately prove to be counterproductive. This is a particularly important point, since waterways can also be used to provide public passenger transport services in built-up areas.

3. POLICY ACTION

Some participants at the Round Table felt that the relatively cursory consideration given to the waterways by policymakers was partly attributable to the fact that the waterways created fewer jobs than, for example, road transport. The emergence of environmental concerns at policy level, however, could help spur renewed interest in the waterways.

The experts at the Round Table felt that the current role of the inland waterways could not be expanded unless charterers' confidence in this mode of transport were restored. This confidence had been eroded by the impossibility of creating long-term ties between the charterer and the carrier, since the chartering by rotation system precluded permanent contractual ties and the emergence of genuine partnerships. Charterers needed to know that they would be dealing with the same parties in the logistical systems they put in place and needed to be able to negotiate the terms and conditions of transport contracts freely without being bound by mandatory tariffs. Lasting relations within a freely negotiated system are essential if charterers are to invest in waterway transport. The abolition of the chartering by rotation system was therefore seen as a positive step by Round Table participants in that the system had not had the positive social impacts foreseen: vessels were still underutilised, with the result that the exclusion of owner-operators had actually been speeded up. At the same time, chartering by rotation had been accompanied by severe restrictions on own-account transport and had therefore slowed the development of the latter.

Germany's experience with tariff liberalisation was considered extremely positive, despite the subsequent fall in tariff levels. The new tariffs were no lower than those charged on international operations -- for which prices had long since been deregulated -- and the fall in prices, which had often been exaggerated, had brought new custom to the waterways. This meant that vessel underutilisation was no longer as serious a problem. In addition, it was common knowledge that mandatory tariffs were frequently an incentive to circumvent the rules, with domestic shipments, for example, being transformed into exports followed by re-imports. Generally speaking, whenever mandatory tariffs have been applied in any transport sector, they have frequently resulted in fraudulent practices. Other restrictions seem to be outdated, such as those prohibiting operation on Sundays and public holidays. They have also had the undesirable effect of limiting waterway competitiveness and should therefore be systematically abolished.

Market liberalisation has increased the number of small operators working as subcontractors to larger firms. It is worth noting in this respect that subcontracting is not necessarily a negative development in that it may prove to be to the advantage of both firms to enter into such an arrangement, even though some forms of contract are not above reproach. It is obviously necessary for the authorities to regulate the types of contractual relations currently emerging by issuing, for example, standard contracts.

Mandatory tariffs had been set up to regulate a market handicapped by seasonal low-water levels that prevent vessels from being fully loaded. Surplus capacity is therefore needed to meet demand in the low-water period. The Round Table considered that an open market would not prevent this extra capacity from being maintained, in keeping with the principles defined by the theory of market uncertainty. The cost of maintaining this extra capacity would be included in the prices which could be freely charged. According to the Round Table participants, it was important to leave matters to the markets and not to interfere with the resulting decisions, even if the transition from regulated to open markets, particularly in the CEECs, might require intermediate stages and specific measures. These measures must form part of a comprehensive

223

transport policy aimed mainly at guaranteeing the competitiveness of operators. In addition, reliance on market mechanisms can only be justified if they are implemented simultaneously in the various countries or, in other words, only if certain national fleets do not benefit from subsidies. Scrapping as a means of adjusting capacity was not considered to be particularly effective since it had been applied indiscriminately to markets. For example, the pursuit of a scrapping policy does not seem desirable on the Rhine. Moreover, since the so-called "scrap and build" regulation had considerably increased fleet productivity, surplus capacity had not been reduced. Capacity can probably be best adjusted by making waterway transport more competitive which, at the same time, would encourage increased demand for inland waterway transport. Shipping companies must therefore be encouraged to modernise their management systems rather than focus on scrapping.

Waterway operators must take a more comprehensive approach to the market. They cannot simply provide haulage but must develop a broader business outlook. This requires greater technical know-how and thus underlines the value of training measures aimed at improving the quality of services provided. Another important step might be to use an appropriate legal framework to stimulate co-operation between waterway operators, as well as between transport modes and between carriers and charterers. This legal framework, which it was primarily the responsibility of the authorities to put in place, should permit the use of bareboat charters, which in many cases had been banned, although they were particularly effective in economic terms. As regards the eastern European countries, it was stressed that the serious restrictions still affecting inland waterway companies, despite extensive privatisation, had to be removed as they were not always consistent with operation in a market economy context. Against this background, there was a need to structure the environment for operators in eastern Europe.

No other form of inland transport is cheaper than the waterway once the cargo is on board. Transshipment costs, however, are high and affect its competitiveness. To reduce these costs, charterers must invest in equipment, which they will do only if they regain confidence in the waterways, meaning if they can establish lasting ties based on freely negotiated conditions. On their side, the operators must opt for innovation, which may require action to promote amalgamations or the creation of co-operatives so that inland waterway transport services are no longer operated as a small-scale business activity.

Public investment in transshipment terminals could be seen as a way of stimulating this mode, but in no case should it exceed 50 per cent of the total cost of the facilities. Moreover, experience has shown that the political authorities should not interfere with decisions on the siting of ports and logistical centres: by and large, this type of investment should remain in the hands of the private sector, which is in a better position to decide whether multimodal facilities involving inland navigation should be set up. At the same time, the focus must be on what already exists rather than on constant striving to create new terminals, as proposed in certain master plans adopted at international level. What is important is to select investments very carefully in order to create a network of river ports, but in some countries this means that disinvestment policies would have to be rejected. The Round Table particularly stressed the need to improve the technical operating conditions on the Danube corridor by increasing draughts and modernising port facilities and fleets. More generally, however, there could be no question of systematically trying to complete networks, since in some cases the investment involved was very high and was not justified by the return on capital, or met with strong opposition on environmental grounds.

If confidence is to be achieved, smooth operation must be guaranteed or, in other words, the current administrative systems must be modified so that regular services can be provided without obstacles due to red tape, customs regulations (particularly on the Danube) and technical problems such as discrepancies in vessel size, resulting in costly transshipments. It is not the aim either to impose an existing convention on certain countries but to find a compromise between the provisions of the Convention of Mannheim and the Treaty of Bratislava. At the same time, it would be particularly advantageous to open up the waterways in the East to foreign operators in order to strengthen their role in the transport of supplies. The ECMT must therefore soon consider the issue of market access for inland navigation and work out common principles in this area.

Inland waterway operators cannot disregard other modes of transport. In this connection, the Round Table participants considered that the road haulage and waterway markets were quite distinct. Competition is, however, very real between rail and inland navigation. The waterways also have much to fear from a resurgence of rail, in particular from the freight freeways, rail privatisation and access by shipping lines to railway networks. Rail will be innovating and cutting its costs, and this will make it more competitive on corridors in which the waterways have a stake. The railways always have scope for cross-subsidising the services they provide, which can make rail extremely competitive on certain links. The competition for container traffic on the Rhine-Main-Danube corridor is perhaps a prime example of this. Inland waterway operators must therefore innovate on the commercial side. Otherwise, it is not sure that the worst will be behind them. The fact that one of the aims of transport policy is to limit growth in the road sector will eventually make the revitalisation of the railways a priority objective, which could damage the outlook for the waterways unless the latter are able to find their own means of enhancing their competitiveness.

The internalisation of external costs was discussed in connection with its possible contribution to modifying the modal split. The answer was that no great change in the modal split can be expected simply as a result of higher road haulage prices. First, the internalisation of external costs is a long-term prospect and, second, road haulage demand no longer seems very sensitive to prices. In addition, waterways are no doubt the transport mode which is the least effective in covering its infrastructure costs, and this will limit the positive effect of internalisation. The waterways will attract new customers rather by developing an aggressive commercial approach, meaning that they should provide not only haulage but full logistical services. Technological innovation by the waterways can be encouraged by the authorities, since charterers will not use a transport mode simply because its prices are quite competitive if the proposed service is not satisfactory in terms of quality. Developing the competitiveness of alternatives to road haulage will also be the best way of protecting the environment. If it transpires that a transport mode cannot develop despite the internalisation of external costs, it may be concluded that the markets are responding to its shortcomings.

CONCLUSIONS

The waterways can make further inroads in established markets and have growth potential on major corridors such as the Danube or in river/maritime transport to and from the Russian Federation. Studies should first of all be conducted to identify this growth potential more clearly, particularly in eastern European countries. To this end, detailed economic analyses need to be carried out, in which markets are broken down both by type of good and by geographical area. In terms of policy action, the lack of harmonized procedures for the routes, which seem vital for the future of waterway transport, can only be deplored. The confidence of charterers in the use of inland waterways must be restored and, in this respect, experience has shown that liberalisation of the sector cannot fail to be beneficial. Excessive regulation has delayed adjustment by the sector to current logistical imperatives. The sector must undoubtedly be helped to progress from the present stage, characterised by an excessively high number of owner-operators, so that better-organised enterprises can be formed through amalgamations and co-operatives. These enterprises will be in a better position to innovate on the commercial side and to withstand competition, primarily from the railways. Genuinely dynamic enterprises must be set up in the CEECs; although state enterprises have been privatised, they still need to learn how to operate in a liberal market economy. By and large, it can be said that the waterways must take the initiative and not expect to simply wait for the costs of other modes to rise. But if it is acceptable to allow the rail sector time to adjust to change and improve competitiveness, then it is only fair to give the waterways time to make progress and introduce the necessary adjustments. At the same time, constant efforts are needed to create a framework within which entrepreneurs can operate while avoiding creating a regulatory regime which will paralyse initiative.

LIST OF PARTICIPANTS

Monsieur Christian PARENT **Chairman**
Directeur Général
Voies Navigables de France (VNF)
175 rue Ludovic Boutleux
F-62408 BETHUNE

Professor Dr. K. BREITZMANN **Rapporteur**
Institut für Verkehr und Logistik
Wirtschafts- und Sozial-Wissenschaftliche Fakultät
Universität Rostock
Schröderstr. 23
D-18051 ROSTOCK

Dr. Christian WENSKE **Co-Rapporteur**
Universität Rostock
Wirtschafts- und Sozialwissenschaftliche Fakultät
Institut für Verkehr und Logistik
Schröderstr. 23
D-18051 ROSTOCK

Madame le Professeur M.-M. DAMIEN **Rapporteur**
Département Logistique et Transport
IUT
22 Allée Jean Rostand
F-91025 EVRY CEDEX

Mr. Pieter HILFERINK
Director of Research
NEA
P.O. Box 1969
NL-2280 DZ RIJSWIJK

Rapporteur

Professor Dr. C. PEETERS
President - Executive Director
Policy Research Corporation NV
Jan Moorkensstraat 68
B-2600 ANTWERPEN (Berchem)

Rapporteur

Dr. Harry WEBERS
Research Associate
Policy Research Corporation N.V.
Jan Moorkensstraat 68
B-2600 ANTWERPEN (Berchem)
Belgique

Co-Rapporteur

Professor Dr. Gerd ABERLE
Justus-Liebig Universität Giessen
Lehrstuhl Volkswirtschaftslehre 1
Licher Strasse 62
D-35394 GIESSEN

M. le Professeur Michel BEUTHE
Facultés Universitaires Catholiques de Mons
151 Chemin de Binche
B-7000 MONS

Monsieur H. DELSAUX
Fédération des Entreprises de Belgique (FEB)
Rue Ravenstein 4
B-1000 BRUXELLES

Mr. Vladimir DIMTCHEV
Managing Director
VECTRA Ltd.
Boulevard Al. Stamboliiski 89-B
BG-1303 SOFIA

Mr. Wouter FREELING
Binnenvaart Nederland
Postbus 23129
NL-3001 KC ROTTERDAM

M. Victor GODIN   **Observer**
Administrateur-Délégué de
l'Institut pour le Transport par Batellerie
Rue de la Presse 19
B-1000 BRUXELLES

Dr. David HILLING
4 Torrington Road
GB-BERKHAMSTED, Herts. HP4 3DD

M. Jean-Claude HOUTMEYERS   **Observer**
1er Conseiller
Ministère des Communications et de l'Infrastructure
ARCI-D2-Résidence Palace
Rue de la Loi 155
B-1040 BRUXELLES

Mlle Chrystelle LAPIERRE   **Observer**
Allocataire de thèse LET/CNR
Compagnie Nationale du Rhône
Service DG - Mission développement
2 rue André-Bonin
F-69316 LYON CEDEX 04

Dr. Dieter LINDENBLATT
Direktor
Thyssen Stahl AG
Kaiser-Wilhelm-Strasse 100
D-47166 DUISBURG

Mr. Viatcheslav NOVIKOV
Economic Affairs Officer
Commission Économique pour l'Europe des Nations Unies
Palais des Nations
8-14 Avenue de la Paix
CH-1211 GENEVE 10

Dr. Erno PÁL
Head of Bureau
Institute for Transport Sciences Limited
Thán K. u. 3-5
P.O.B. 107
H-1518 BUDAPEST

M. Yves PARMENTIER   **Observer**
Conseiller général a.i.
Ministère des Communications et de l'Infrastructure
Administration du Transport Terrestre
Cantersteen 12
B-1000 BRUXELLES

Mr. Peter SCHNEIDEWIND
Director
Austrian Institute for Regional Studies and Spatial Planning
Franz-Josefs-Kai 27
A-1010 WIEN

Dr. Viktor SIEGL
Ministerialrat
Bundesministerium für Wissenschaft und Verkehr
Verwaltungsbereich Verkehr
als Oberate Schiffahrtsbehörde
Radetzkystrasse 2
A-1031 WIEN

Madame Marie-Dominique SIMONET
Directeur-Général
Port Autonome de Liège
Quai de Maestricht 14
B-4000 LIEGE

Professor Jan SIMONS
Secretary
Chambre de Commerce
P.O. 30025
NL-3001 DA ROTTERDAM

Dr. László UGRÓCZKY
Közlekedési Tanszék
Széchenyi István Föiskola
Közlekedési és Gépészmérnöki Fakultás
Pf. 701
H-9007 GYOR

Drs. Peter VAN DALEN
Ministerie van Verkeer en Waterstaat
Directie Vervoersectoren
Afdeling Binnenvaart
Postbus 20904
NL-2500 EX DEN HAAG

Dipl.-Ökonom. Wolfgang VOLLMER
Managing Director
Nestrans Logistik GmbH
Kasteelstrasse 2
D-47119 DUISBURG

Monsieur Hans van der WERF   **Observer**
Secrétaire Général Adjoint
Commission Centrale pour la Navigation du Rhin
2 Place de la République
Palais du Rhin
67082 STRASBOURG CEDEX

ECMT SECRETARIAT

Mr. Gerhard AURBACH – Secretary-General

ECONOMIC RESEARCH, STATISTICS AND DOCUMENTATION DIVISION

Mr. Alain RATHERY – Head of Division

Mr. Michel VIOLLAND - Administrator

Mrs Julie PAILLIEZ - Assistant

Ms Françoise ROULLET - Assistant

TRANSPORT POLICY DIVISION

Mrs Sophie FOUVEZ - Principal Administrator

ALSO AVAILABLE

Changing Daily Urban Mobility: Less or Differently?. Series ECMT - Round Table 102 (1996)
(75 96 06 1) ISBN 92-821-1216-0   France FF260   £34   US$50   DM76

The Separation of Operations from Infrastructure in the Provision of Railway Services. Series ECMT - Round Table 103 (1997)
(75 97 02 1P) ISBN 92-821-1221-7   France FF295   £38   US$58   DM86

New Trends in Logistics in Europe - Round Table 104 (1997)
(75 97 05 1 P) ISBN 92-821-1224-1   France FF215   £28 $US42   DM63

Infrastructure-Induced Mobility. Series ECMT - Round Table 105 (1998)
(75 98 07 1 P) ISBN 92-821-1232-2   France FF400   £40 $US67   DM119

Intercity Transport markets in Countries in Transition. Series ECMT - Round Table 106 (1998)
(75 98 10 1 P) ISBN 92-821-1235-7   France FF400   £41 $US66   DM119

User charges for railway Infrastructure. Series ECMT – Round Table 107 (1998)
(75 98 14 1 P) ISBN 92-821-1240-3   France FF290   £30 $US50   DM86

14th International Symposium on Theory and Practice in Transport Economics. Which Changes for Transport in the Next Century? (1999)
(75 1999 01 1 P) ISBN 92-821-1241-1 France FF590   £63 $US105   DM176

Prices charged at the OECD Bookshop.

*The OECD CATALOGUE OF PUBLICATIONS and supplements will be sent free of charge
on request addressed either to OECD Publications Service,
or to the OECD Distributor in your country.*

OECD PUBLICATIONS, 2, rue André-Pascal, 75775 PARIS CEDEX 16
PRINTED IN FRANCE
(75 1999 06 1 P) ISBN 92-821-1246-2 – No.50659 1999